Whatever happened to the
TEENAGE
DREAM?

Postcards from the edge of 80s pop

Whatever happened to the
TEENAGE DREAM?

Postcards from the edge of 80s pop

a Memoir by

Dan Synge

For Chris Gausden, 1963-1985

CONTENTS

"The languor of Youth – how unique and quintessential it is!
How quickly, how irrevocably, lost!
The zest, the generous affections, the illusions, the despair, all the
traditional attributes of Youth – all save this – come and go with us
through life."

Evelyn Waugh (*Brideshead Revisited*, 1945)

I'm not your Hoochie Coochie Man, I'm not the Seventh Son,
Just another middle-class white boy,
I'm tryin' to have some fun

Mose Allison (*Middle Class White Boy*, 1982)

Guess this world needs its dreamers
May they never wake up (alright!)

Prefab Sprout (*Cars and Girls*, 1988)

PROLOGUE:
THAT'S ME IN THE CORNER

So what got *you* into pop music? And why, for that matter, are you still listening to it?

Casting my eyes around the room where I write this, I spy at least three six-stringed solid-bodied electric guitars. One of them leans against a small amplifier by the window. Two more hang side by side on a wall as if they were on display in my favourite Denmark Street music shop. A recently acquired bass guitar rests against the bookshelf to my left and above the coat rack by the door is a mini analogue synthesizer in its original box. Alongside it are several other electric keyboards and some portable drum machines. In their day, they would have been at the cutting edge of music technology.

Rows of vinyl albums going back to the 1980s and beyond still occupy a dusty corner on the floor and, behind me, are some shelves dedicated to collected rock journalism and music biographies. Used and unused tickets for various live shows jostle for space on the mantlepiece – Spiritualized, First Aid Kit, Goldfrapp, and The Jim Jones All Stars, a superb live band who I've seen twice already. And why not? With their loud, distorted guitars and 'shake a tail feather' horn section, they sound like the bastard offspring of The Stooges and The James Brown Revue.

Next to the very computer I'm typing this out on is a random collection of CDs (yes CDs, popularly in use forty years ago) and, resting on the floor below, are a decent enough pair of audio speakers through which I can hear my favourite new artists. Strangely, I've been as enthusiastic about releases by The Surfing Magazines, Daniel Romano's Outfit, Nightbus, Jane Weaver and Wet Leg (or indeed anything on their producer Dan Carey's Speedy Wunderground label) as when I first heard *No More Heroes* or *Love Will Tear Us Apart* as a wide-eyed teenager.

But why, oh why I wonder, do I still feel the pull of this damned music? What can possibly be the attraction? Why doesn't it all just f-f-f-fade away?

When rock and roll first exploded into the consciousness back in the 1950s, it was an exclusively teenage obsession; a silly, visceral fad that the adults or the 'squares' believed would quickly go the way of the Hula-Hoop or the conical bra. Now, having been fully absorbed into the mainstream, it's no longer a badge of youth or rebellion. Instead, it's just a lazy cultural comfort blanket for a generation of Baby Boomers and Generation X-ers born roughly between 1960 and 1985.

Including myself in this once relevant social demographic, I can assure you that more recent music genres like Grime and K-pop pass by virtually unnoticed when you're busy revisiting Nancy & Lee or arguing in the pub the case for *Neat, Neat, Neat* being the best punk record ever recorded.

And if you thought rock audiences were getting younger, have you seen the number of greying or balding punters who congregate regularly at our favourite music temples: The Roundhouse, Brixton Academy and the 100 Club?

Oh, and by the way, that's me alone in the corner, often deridingly known as '6 Music Dad' cradling an overpriced craft Pale Ale and remembering the time I was there back in 1983, while my teenage daughter goes mental with her mates at the front.

The story you are about to read, therefore, is a personal, cathartic and occasionally humorous examination of the continuing hold that popular music has had on myself and, it would seem, many others like me.

This is not just another lurid tale of adolescent misadventures or the rose-tinted memory of a vainglorious assault on the daunting rock hegemony, although I'll be able to fill these chapters in easily enough. Nor is it simply a nostalgic return to a distant 1970s childhood and the hedonistic 1980s which, incidentally, is now as far away as World War Two was when we were getting into Adam and the Ants and The Smiths.

Whatever happened to the teenage dream? asked Marc Bolan on his eponymous 1974 single, an epic Toni Visconti production that conjured up a post-pop dystopia overshadowed by the deaths of James Dean and Marilyn Munroe, plus a litany of tragic rock and roll stars from Buddy and Eddie through to Jimi, Janis and Jim.

I once had such a dream and, by the end of this coming-of-age tale that has been touched ineffably by music both good and bad, I want to fully explore and understand, with return visits to some of the most significant moments of my mis-spent youth, how it ever came about.

I will examine, with an almost forensic approach, the ordinary and the extraordinary, the cool and the uncool, the transient and the lasting. I will weave seemingly disconnected memories into one clear and redemptive whole. And, who knows, maybe my findings will help to explain why I always get goosebumps whenever I hear the opening guitar riff to T Rex's *Ride A White Swan*.

London, 2024

1.

WATERLOO

The living room curtains are drawn and I'm sitting cross legged in front of the family television set. There's a pile of Twiglets in a bowl by my feet and, on a nearby antique side table, a glistening box of Terry's All Gold. Next to it is a glass of chilled Babycham.

These are for the exclusive consumption of Mrs Fitzgerald, a retired post mistress from the village, who is my companion for the evening.

Mrs Fitzgerald normally came in on Fridays to do the hoovering for my mum but, on this most special of Saturday nights, she had made something of an effort with her fluffy woollen cardigan and powdered face obscured partly by a pair of tortoiseshell cat eye spectacles.

I had already had my hot bath and the rather hurried beans on toast. Like a miniaturised Hugh Hefner, I had slicked my hair back and changed into my oversized red dressing gown. I was all set for the long night ahead. This, after all, was the nineteenth edition of the Eurovision Song Contest, the competition launched in 1956 to promote peace and harmony through music and culture among the war-ravaged European nations.

"Ladies and gentlemen, mesdames et messieurs…Katie Boyle!"

Our compere, the former Camay soap model and undisputed queen of received pronunciation, stepped out from the wings to face the live studio audience inside Brighton's historic Dome.

"This contest is being transmitted to more than 32 countries so something like 500 million people are watching at this very moment, as well as the many millions who are listening to their radios all over Europe."

We couldn't help but marvel at Miss Boyle's shiny salmon pink number which contrasted with the regimented black-tie approach of the middle-aged VIP's who occupied the stalls.

"Doesn't she look lovely!" said Mrs Fitzgerald, helping herself to a rum truffle from the plain gold box.

"Yes," I replied. "Do you think she's going to introduce The Wombles soon, Mrs Fitzgerald? They're my favourite!"

A mouth-watering 17 countries including the newly admitted Greece were having their songs aired, but before we got to hear any of what Katie called the "specially composed entries", we were treated to a short film about the host town. The south coast resort of Brighton, it transpired, was a last-minute replacement for Luxembourg who had to decline the opportunity to host the event for financial reasons.

This was 1974 after all, a year in which the entire western world suffered an almighty recession in the wake of the global oil and economic crisis, driving up the price of crude oil by an unprecedented 300% in the process. Here in Britain, the outgoing Prime Minister Edward Heath brought in an emergency three day working week to counter the actions of striking unions and to help conserve our stock of coal. In those days coal, and coal alone, fuelled the nation's electric power stations.

Operating restrictions were also imposed on our three television channels. Until just recently, broadcasts had to end by 10.30pm every night. Chaos and candles seemed to be an overriding theme of early 1974.

Anyway, first up was a young lady from Finland with a forgettable song called *Keep Me Warm*, then it was the turn of Olivia Newton-John with our entry *Long Live Love*. The United Kingdom had some form at the *Grand Prix Eurovision de la Chanson Européenne*; Dagenham born Sandie Shaw won in 1967 with *Puppet On A String* while the pint-sized Scottish songstress Lulu repeated the feat two years later with *Boom Bang-a-Bang*.

"Oh, I do like *her*," remarked Mrs Fitzgerald, as a striking-looking blonde twiddled a mauve parasol in the gardens outside the Dome.

"Yeah, she looks nice," I replied, before spearing the last of the spicy Twiglets into my gullet.

We then watched our hotly tipped contestant take the stage in a floor-length sky-blue dress.

"What a lovely smile she has," opined Mrs Fitzgerald, warming quickly to the 26-year-old from Melbourne, Australia. Miss Newton-John was then a good five years away from being cast as high school sweetheart Sandy in *Grease* and several more before she was seen gyrating provocatively in a leotard for the *Let's Get Physical* video.

As the band struck up the tune, Miss Newton-John began by swinging her arms to the steady beat:

Long, long live love
Love is to care
Caring and sharing
Long, long live love

Even at the tender age of ten, I could tell that this number was little more than a chorus masquerading as a fully composed piece of music. Still, she was singing it for us and, quite possibly, the fast-sinking reputation of our country abroad. Britain's disappointing economic performance was just one of the reasons we had only recently been allowed into the EEC (European Economic Community). An initial application to be part of the free trade area was rejected in 1960, and it would take a further 13 years before we were fully admitted into the club.

Looking over to the comfiest armchair I could see that Mrs Fitzgerald's slippers were tapping away contentedly to the beat. Assisted by some rather matronly looking backing singers behind her, Miss Newton-John had gone into the final key change before taking the hearty applause from the stalls and circle areas. Her radiant smile, aided by a set of perfect white teeth, seemed to be telling us viewers at home: "Don't worry about the Germans, the Spanish or the Swiss, we've got this."

Admittedly, it was way too early at this point of the transmission to predict a British triumph, but as we sat through Spanish flamenco guitars, a Greek bouzouki inspired offering and the dreadful Poogy, a tanked-topped sextet from Israel, it was looking as if the night might belong to our Olivia.

"When are The Wombles on?" I asked Mrs Fitzgerald, trying to stifle a yawn. The last thing I wanted was to be sent to bed early.

"The Wombles? What the devil is that?"

"You've never heard of The Wombles? They're brilliant Mrs Fitzgerald! They're like a proper rock band with guitars but they pick up the rubbish in the park and they've got this song that goes 'underground, overground, wombling free, The Wombles of Wimbledon Common are we…' Please, please let me stay up for The Wombles!"

"Well, your mum says you're supposed to be in bed by the time they get back from the steak house. Let's see, shall we?"

She took another sip of her Babycham. I bet she had had no truck with troublemakers in the queue at her post office.

To be honest, if it hadn't been for the prospect of Mike Batt's furry eco warriors, scheduled to appear during that segment when all the votes were totted up, I would have left Mrs Fitzgerald to her dark chocolate assortment right there and then. But an eighth act was being introduced.

"We're looking at Sweden, a country full of mountains, lakes and forests…and, of course, it's full of blonde Vikings," began the David Vine voiceover in the pre-recorded segment designed, presumably, to showcase the eccentricities of every artist from these far-flung European corners.

"These are the ABBA group," continued Vine, "Björn, Frida (sic), Anna (sic) just beside her with the long blonde hair and…Benny."

Then, as the screen cut to the live broadcast in Brighton, we watched Sven-Olof Walldoff enter the orchestra pit to rousing cheers. "Oh, and it's Napoleon!" exclaimed Vine, otherwise a *Ski Sunday* and *Superstars* presenter, remarking on the conductor's distinctive bicorne hat and frock coat ensemble. One can only imagine the *froideur* of any French contingent who happened to be watching. They may not have found the joke quite so amusing. But with France's entry having been withdrawn in respect of their recently deceased President Georges Pompidou, an international incident had at least been avoided.

The live studio cameras had now panned across to the stage, where the as-yet-still-unknown band of Vikings were ready to go.

Bearded Benny sat behind the grand piano. His mate, Björn, was positioned on the far side wearing silver boots and hunched troll-like over a matching custom electric guitar shaped like a star.

"Watch this one," said Vine before a simple one note rock guitar riff kicked the Swedish entry into life. Two female singers then raced to front of the stage like mums in an egg and spoon race – a sparkling riot of hair, velvet and glitter – before launching into their alternative history lesson. Little did we know at the time, but this was a moment that would change the course of late-20th century popular music:

My, my – BOOM! – at Waterloo Napoleon did surrender…

From my position on the burgundy carpet next to Mrs Fitzgerald's armchair, my first impression was that for a pop group they all looked a little on the mature side and, indeed, not far off the age of my own parents, who must have been close to forty then.

The two women in the group seemed remarkably beautiful and had noticeably good hair and teeth – not always a given for popular entertainers in the 1970s. I edged a little bit closer to the screen.

Very quickly I was swept along by the catchy saxophone-driven beat and the irresistible chorus with its – to my ears – nonsensical refrain *'Waterloo, how would you feel if you won the war?'* Only decades later would I learn they were in fact singing the line: *'Waterloo, I was defeated, you won the war'.*

Misheard lyrics would continue to blight my enjoyment of pop – notably the maddening 'wrapped up like a douche' from *Blinded By The Light* or The Police's punk/reggae tribute to the BBC newsreader 'Sue Lawley'. Whatever was being lost in translation that night, this ten-year-old child and his retired postmistress chum had forgotten all about golden girl Olivia and were now rooting firmly for the Swedes. Yes, the Swedes!

"Blimey that was good!" said Mrs Fitzgerald, clapping her hands together while flashing an enormous grin. Mrs Fitzgerald's default look was grumpy old widow. I had never seen her smile like this before. So Mrs Fitzgerald was human after all.

Of course, the evening's entertainment was far from done and it would be another hour at least until The Wombles were allowed their moment in the spotlight. Somehow, however, it felt the competition had already been concluded.

Mrs Fitzgerald and I dutifully sat through a procession of dreary piano ballads, some neo-folk posturing and Holland's entry *I See A Star*, which featured a sort of crude barrel organ from which some disturbing looking puppets protruded. Each of these acts seemed utterly pointless after the game-changing brilliance of *Waterloo*.

The Wombles eventually got to do their thing at the pier and at various other Brighton landmarks and, of course, Sweden ran away with *La Grand Prix* with a whopping 24 points.

The ice cool multilinguist Miss Boyle even dropped the *sang-froid* to call the Swedes back for one final rendition of *Waterloo*.

"They say they're shocked at having won, I don't believe it for a minute," added the plummy BBC Director-General standing next to her.

By this stage I could barely keep my eyes open, but even I could tell that ABBA's closing performance was an altogether different beast to their more controlled version earlier on in the show.

Frida nearly garrotted herself with a stray microphone lead as she attempted to climb through the tiny hatch that opened onto the illuminated concert stage. Then there were the barely restrained tears of joy on Agnetha's face as she swung her hips one more time to this instant pop masterpiece. Still cheering them along at home, Mrs Fitzgerald and I witnessed the first of a few soon-to-be trademark faceoffs between the girls. As the polite English applause rang out once again, the blonde bombshell Agnetha planted an affectionate kiss on husband Björn's cheek. What a night!

With the tune still ringing in my ears I crept up to my bedroom and drifted off to sleep.

Make no mistake, this was one of pop's defining moments, comparable to the time when a puppyish Elvis Presley sauntered into Sun Studios, Memphis, to record *That's Alright Mama*. Comparable to that nano-second when Bowie put a thin white arm around guitarist Mick Ronson during a chorus of *Starman* on *Top of the Pops*. Comparable to Nirvana going absolutely berserk on *The Word*.

And for me, I had discovered there was now another group as good as The Beatles, who tragically had broken up four years earlier. And, as if to prove my allegiance to this new Scandi pop sensation, the very next day I began to painstakingly draw and colour in a poster-sized homage to the group detailing both their incredible silver platform boots and Benny's unfeasibly shaped guitar. Where on earth do you get a guitar like that? I wondered.

Not even Dave Hill from Slade, notorious for his collection of unconventional axes including his custom built 'Super Yob', could come up with something so damn flashy.

Before a critical re-evaluation of their back catalogue in the mid-1990s, ABBA with their colour co-ordinated jump suits and cheesy Euro disco melodies would become the epitome of uncool. If you were into real rock music, you just wouldn't go there.

But, for now, nothing was going to stop these Scandi super troupers on their victorious march into pop legend.

2.

BOLERO

"Are you a rat? You look like a rat."

I lay stock still on the iron bed with my head on the pillow waiting for lights out.

"Well…*are* you a rat?"

No one had ever asked me this before. I thought long and hard about how I should answer this, but the question seemed so ridiculous that, in the end, I went along with what I presumed was a bit of harmless leg pulling.

"Yes," I replied eventually.

A horrible smirk then came over the older boy's pale freckled face (actually, Kennedy looked a lot like a rodent himself) as he stood up and announced to his audience of a dozen pyjama-clad ten-year-olds.

"Listen everybody. Synge says that he's a rat. Ha, ha, ha, ha!"

The warm afterglow of my musical epiphany with Katie Boyle and her swanky crowd at Brighton's Dome was cruelly overshadowed by the fact that I soon had to return to my prep school. Yet again, I would be at the mercy of the staff and at least half a dozen rotten eggs among my fellow boarders, holed up in a red-bricked, neo-Elizabethan mansion some 20 miles inland from the Sussex coast off the newly built M23.

Journeying further into the heart of mid-1970s popular culture would be nigh on impossible, and soon the joyful, celebratory sound of ABBA and, to a lesser extent The Wombles, would fade to austere silence.

Other than the fact that there was no telephone, no television and no pop records, pop weeklies or pop annuals lying around the communal areas (the super-swotty *Look and Learn* with its focus on space travel and medieval castles was the only approved weekly), we were all dispatched to bed by 8pm.

More often than not, the children's classic *Sparky's Magic Piano* – an unlikely story about a boy whose talking piano turns him into a musical prodigy – was played over an old intercom before lights out. The only other music we heard before bedtime was Maurice Ravel's *Bolero* which, with its exotic Latin American rhythms that built slowly but surely to an orchestral crescendo that critics liken to sexual climax, seemed an odd choice by the headmaster. I'm no prude, but as a soothing bedtime melody, *Bolero* with its bombastic *finale* of cymbal crashes and neighing horns just didn't seem appropriate for children's bedtime.

Indeed, by the time *Waterloo* was sitting comfortably at the top of the 'hit parade', my indoctrination into the school's rigid and unsentimental ideology was practically complete. Dispatched there shortly after turning eight, I was like the peace-loving hippy who had been drafted into fighting the Viet Cong and found, to their surprise, they were a cold-blooded killer.

Admittedly, my initiation two years earlier had been tough, both physically and mentally. It involved being subjected to repeated abuse by our dorm monitors, a pair of brutal tyrants who could hardly have been twelve years old themselves.

Whether it was the terrifying whip crack of a dressing gown cord or a heavy thump to the head from a club fashioned from a wet bath towel, we simply took these random punishments in our stride.

There was no mummy to hold our hand, no comforting cuddle and no Penguin chocolate biscuit to help wipe away our tears. Instead, there was an angry, white-coated matron we called 'Pig Nut'.

This woman, who was supposed to be our leading adult safeguard with our health and mental well-being at the core of her daily routine, simply ignored these regular beatings, which took place on Sunday mornings as the staff slept in. Instead, she would chide those poor wretches who wet their beds or sobbed uncontrollably into their pillow each night for being so noisy and selfish.

It was remarkable how quickly I transitioned from being an easy-going eight-year-old with a loving family, a chubby black and white cat and primary school teachers who in their final report described me as 'an endearing and able child' with a natural talent for English and Art, to this quiet and introverted Maths dunderhead intent simply on survival. On the outside I was a smart freckled schoolboy in regulation grey. Inside, I felt like a character from the childhood game Picture Consequences, a discombobulated mess of a space explorer's body, dragoon guard's trousers and the grinning head of a chimpanzee.

John Lennon famously sang *'imagine no possessions, I wonder if you can'*. At this place, Lennon's neo-Marxist concept was easy to relate to; not because I didn't have any worldly goods, but because all records, toys, magazines, gadgets or items of personal clothing we brought into the school were unceremoniously confiscated and often never to be seen again.

Missing in action during that traumatic first term included some irreplaceable family photos and, arguably more soul-destroying, my lifelong confidante Merrythought Mouse. For no obvious reason other than malice, a sour-faced ruffian called Oliver ejected him through a gap in our classroom window and into the bushes outside.

The teacher, a seemingly kind lady called Mrs Reeves, refused even to allow me permission to delve into the rhododendrons to retrieve my faithful furry friend. Somewhere in the school, I reckoned there must have been a secret door behind which lay my lost property alongside some mailbags of cash from the Great Train Robbery and possibly even an unshaven Lord Lucan dressed in a silk dressing gown.

In hindsight, this unsettling passage of my life could, I suppose, be credited for some of the resilience and stoicism I have shown in later years. 'Out of life's school of war – what doesn't kill me makes me stronger', so Nietzsche's saying goes.*

Twilight of the Idols, 1889.

But what, I sometimes wonder, did I miss out on by going along with this cruel and cold charade that played out, no doubt, in provincial boarding schools throughout the land during the 1970s and possibly even later?

The everyday physical and emotional love of my mother and father would be the first that springs to mind, and it puzzles me even today why such warm, sensitive and easy-going parents like mine would have considered signing up for such a thing.

I mean, they subscribed to *The Guardian!* They voted either Labour or Liberal and had a large photo of Shirley Williams (cut out from the pages of *The Guardian*) pinned to our kitchen wall.

But even more unfair was the fact that as I sat through evening prep or lay there subjected to *Sparky's Magic Piano* for the umpteenth time with its nauseating '*sit down on my stool, press your fingers on my keys*', my friends back home would no doubt be feasting on the latest television comedy sketches by Monty Python and The Goodies.

Some may have even been sipping home-made cola from their mum's SodaStream drinks maker or trading bubble gum cards depicting hirsute footballers. Others would, no doubt, be packing away their Scalextric or Hot Wheels sets. The lucky sods.

Major world events such as Bloody Sunday, the end of the Vietnam War, England's humiliation by Poland* or the release of Bowie's *Aladdin Sane* didn't stand a chance against hardy school perennials such as rugger, cricket ball throwing (a sort of javelin substitute that featured only on Sport's Day) and, starting as early as April, swimming bollock naked in a murky newt filled pond.

The quaintly named 'duck pond' turned out to be a mere gateway for entering the enormous natural lake it had been constructed directly alongside and looked suspiciously as if a local farmer might have dragged his sheep through it. Only when we could prove our

---

* **Poland, or rather their acrobatic goalkeeper Jan Tomaszewski denied England qualification to the 1974 World Cup at Wembley in October 1973. Needing only a win to beat the Poles, Alf Ramsey's side could only manage a 1-1 draw. In the pre-match build up, TV pundit Brian Clough had called the unruly-haired Tomaszewski 'a circus clown in gloves'.**

ability by swimming the required twenty lengths of this pitch-black pool, overseen by the batshit crazy science master, Mr Dibley, were we allowed to cover up and join the lucky bathers in the lake.

Relief came from attending a Saturday afternoon scale modelling workshop which was supervised, it must be commended, by a genuine former Wing Commander we called 'The Winco'. Naturally, he wore an immaculate double-breasted Prince of Wales check suit and sported a magnificent handlebar moustache. On one occasion he insisted that I completely re-paint the matt white undercarriage of my 1:72 scale Mosquito dive bomber with the colour duck egg blue. Seeing that he had probably flown the damn things, there wasn't much room for argument.

Mr Arnold, a Maths teacher who ran the Colts XI football team as well as a fortnightly stamp collecting club, was another adult worth looking up to. Every Saturday afternoon he would ramp up the drama of our much-anticipated philatelic happenings by depositing random Penny Blacks and their poorer cousins, the Penny Reds, into trays of stamps that originated from all corners of the world.

Spotting a degree of talent in my performance playing in midfield, he even gave me a shot at being a centre forward for the Colts XI. In my untucked plain blue shirt and Gola Speedster boots, I dreamt of dictating the game with incisive long passes and canny goalmouth assists, but in the match itself I barely managed to get possession of the ball, let alone hit the back of the net.

It was impossible to imagine such louche hedonism but, as I eagerly chased leather in the mud or searched for rare Victorian stamps, in an altogether different universe Marc Bolan's seminal LP *The Slider* was being released and the 'Unholy Trinity' of David, Iggy and Lou were being immortalised by photographer-cum-glam courtier Mick Rock at London's Dorchester Hotel. But unlike Ziggy with his endless costume changes and high maintenance make up routine, we had to stay in our grey flannelled shorts all year round. Our hair, meanwhile, was kept regulation short thanks to a barber from Redhill who would visit the school each term to give every boy the very same boring haircut.

Glam rock, the movement which started when an androgenous-looking Bolan appeared with glitter-strewn cheeks on an episode of *Top of the Pops* in March 1971, had to my dismay coincided with this most hard-core approach to schooling.

Is it any wonder that bands such as Mott The Hoople, The New York Dolls and Roxy Music almost completely passed me by?

Roxy's 1973 album *Stranded* with the critically acclaimed *Street Life, Mother of Pearl* and *A Song For Europe* had a cover featuring glamorous *Playboy* model, Marilyn Cole, in a distressed red Antony Price dress. The album's title could equally have expressed my sense of abandonment here in the home counties.

In essence, the lives of the 130 or so pupils residing here were no different to those who experienced the school fifty years earlier and possibly even fifty years before that. We were in a time capsule, stuck approximately in the year 1924.

The overpowering smell of floor wax meets over-boiled cabbage and the ghostly black and white group photos that lined the passageway which led to the oppressive stained wood dining room were chilling proof of that.

The sepia-tinted portraits of the truly old boys had a haunting effect on me. Those lost souls posing stiffly in ancient team line ups and holding stitched leather footballs with the year chalked in white stared back at me as if to say: "Live your life while you can."

Some of them would have grown up only to meet terrible ends at one or other of the World War One hellscapes. My suspicions weren't entirely the stuff of morbid fantasy as my great uncle Edward – a character, who for one reason or another, had been airbrushed from my own family's history – had vanished in the mud at Cambrai, aged only eighteen.

It didn't help that I was a naturally shy and sensitive child, completely untrained in the art of fighting my corner and standing up to abuse. Just to give you an idea of how much of a shrinking violet I was, Mrs Reeves asked me to conduct the junior triangle orchestra at the annual Christmas concert. The entire school and their parents were to attend.

All seemed to go swimmingly in rehearsals as I waved my baton convincingly enough to the plodding infantile rhythm, but on the night itself I froze.

I'm not and never really have been comfortable in the spotlight and standing up there on that stage, I simply couldn't bear to look up into those rows of faces with their cold, judgmental eyes. I chose instead to focus on my regulation black leather shoes and the plain wooden boards directly below. How I wished they would swallow me up. In this paralysed and panic-ridden state I could barely lift up my arms and face the various band members around me who were, to be fair, gamely doing their best to reach the end. Put it this way, I was no Leonard Bernstein or Herbert von Karajan.

Naturally, the after-show teasing was merciless. "Your conducting was superb, Synge, will you be doing it next year?" remarked some of the older boys. Each of them followed up their hilarious critique by doing an impression of my awkward, floor-bound cranium.

Shortly afterwards, I found myself in a new dorm sleeping next to a boy named Kennedy, the monitor responsible for us having tidy beds and for being tucked up in time for pre-lights out reading. This was also the boy who told me I looked like a rat.

Actually, I didn't mind being called a rat. I would be called worse things than that, here and at other institutions. But bizarrely this boy continued to keep his insistent line of questioning going weeks and even months after I had first confessed to my newfound rodent status.

"Are you a rat?" a familiar voice came from the other side of the urinal.

Oh, here goes, it's that weirdo Kennedy again.

"Yes, I *am* a rat, can't you bloody well see!"

3.

THAT'LL BE THE DAY

"So what is *this* young Synge? Am I to understand you are in the process of reading some kind of comic?"

The headmaster held up my copy of *Asterix In Britain* for all to see.

"No, sir."

"Oh, so it's a work of literature that we see before us! Something to rank alongside the great works of Chaucer or Shakespeare?"

Some of the other boys in the dorm chuckled.

He examined the pages of my illustrated story about Asterix the plucky Gallic warrior and his mad cap plan to deliver a magic potion to the tea drinking Brits from the other side of the Channel, thereby helping to usurp the entire Roman Empire.

"What rubbish!" he harrumphed, hurling the offending tome back onto the bed's counterpane. "Why don't you read proper books like Fraser here?"

Fraser held up his paperback copy of *HMS Ulysses* with a detectable smirk.

"Alistair MacLean. Excellent choice, Fraser, and yours, Waterhouse. The Hornblower series is superb. CS Forester's books are beautifully written and capture all the excitement of life at sea during the Napoleonic Wars. Asterix In Britain – I mean, *honestly!* Well gentlemen, it's practically lights out."

The relentless erosion of our individuality was certainly cruel and demeaning, but the tactic was undeniably effective as a sort of safeguard against the incursions of modern cultural life. If Soviet leaders could prohibit bubble gum, Levi's blue jeans and Elvis and Chuck Berry records during the Cold War years, our teachers could probably keep glam rock and the collected works of Goscinny and Uderzo at bay.

A monthly Sunday afternoon outing to our parents' or, if invited, to the home of another boy, allowed us an all-too brief glimpse of the world outside. The short time spent with mum and dad was priceless, yet it was the shiny and superfluous things that mattered most.

Trying hard to adjust to this alien domestic scene, I settled in front of the telly and gorged on choc ices and Cresta sparkling orange while a pair of playboy sleuths, *The Persuaders!*, swanned around the Côte d'Azur in an Aston Martin*. *The Big Match* delivered thrills and spills in equal measure, but with the wintry quagmires of Stoke, Wolverhampton and Burnley as the backdrop. I had to admire those football 'fancy Dans' with their shaggy feather cuts or terrible comb overs as they danced over the mud to avoid being kicked senseless by a succession of 1970s football hard men. And after a Sunday roast and a kick about with friends in the park, it was practically time to head back down the motorway.

I fought back the tears as we cruised along the Brighton Road towards our destination, the only distraction being Alan Freeman's gripping chart run down which ended at the school gates. I wouldn't say he spoiled it exactly, but as the face of the Brentford Nylons television commercials ('top quality polyester sheets in prints and plain') The Radio 1 DJ, aka 'Fluff', had played an all-too-prominent role in my big day out.

Occasionally, I would be collected by my grandmother who everyone in my family called Grannie Squirrel. A widower, whose husband had served in the trenches and later in the civil service, she

---

*The harpsichord intro to *The Persuaders!* theme by John Barry was a clarion call for pre-pubescent boys to finish up their grub and monopolise the family television set.

lived just the other side of Horsham in a house that overlooked the cricket green. Her only son, my dad, was evacuated to America during World War Two so she missed much of his childhood.

I felt she was making up for this as she spoiled me rotten with all the things that were denied me at school; Cadbury's chocolate bars, plump Wall's sausages and instant Smash potato granules that were washed down with bowl after bowl of butterscotch Angel Delight.

During those painfully short autumn and winter afternoons, she would laugh and gossip over tea and Mr Kipling cakes with her friend The Management (another local widow with a funny name) and a lady called Pat who looked and spoke remarkably like a man and who went fishing, drank real ale and smoked filter-less Player's Navy Cut cigarettes. Mrs Fletcher, who lived next door, had a kind round face and spoke with a beautiful West Sussex burr.

While grannie served up tea or, later in the evening, huge tumblers of bourbon on ice, I would make myself comfortable on her pale green shag pile and set to work on my latest Action Transfer booklet sourced from a toy shop in nearby Billingshurst.

Produced either by Patterson Blick or Letraset, a company who otherwise produced typefaces on small plastic sheets, these booklets offered introspective children like me a fun, interactive entrée into key historical moments, from the Romans and the Vikings to more recent events like D-Day and the Battle of Britain.

It took a firm hand indeed and a smooth Biro or pencil, not to mention the positioning of a solid hardback book underneath, to apply the action figures accurately to the blank panoramas within. But with enough concentration and extra helpings of Cresta orangeade – 'it's frothy man!' – the double page spread would soon be populated with tanks, wagons, horses or soldiers (living, dead or dying) as the Charge of The Light Brigade or the Battle for The Alamo came to life in front of my eyes.

To me, the appeal of these illustrated books was the satisfaction of task completion and, of course, Grannie Squirrel would offer sincere congratulations on a job well done, usually with another of Mr Kipling's 'exceedingly good cakes'.

Deciding who wins Waterloo or whether Hannibal and his elephants cross The Alps or not is of course the ultimate exercise in control. In my case, it was simply a way of shutting out the unwanted noise of conformity and competition; an all-too-brief respite from the relentless demands of school and its unforgiving curriculum.

Having been dropped back in time for Sunday evening chapel, I would well up and cry into my prayer book, especially when the opening chords to *Eternal Father, Strong to Save* struck up on the organ. Why did hymns have to be so grim? The ancient anthem inspired by Psalm 107 had had a similar effect, when aged seven, I attended my grandfather's funeral in a tiny Herefordshire chapel. To me it spelled out the harsh reality that one day our loved ones and, inevitably, we ourselves would perish like those poor mariners in the tumultuous 'ocean deep'.

O hear us when we cry to Thee
For those in peril on the sea

But boys like me, who lived an hour and a half away and had happy and loving homes to go back to, were in fact the lucky ones.

Less fortunate were those whose parents had permanently cast them out leaving them here like survivors of a shipwreck; the ones whose family roots were in Hong Kong, Kenya, Bermuda, India and other posts of our former Empire. Some of these poor souls may have even hailed from Surrey.

I will never forget the boy who, even when careering through the school's many corridors, almost always had his nose pressed inside a book. Naturally, we called him 'Bookworm'.

Or Charlesworth, the podgy older boy whose father's sudden death was announced in school assembly. I should have said something kind and reassuring to Charlesworth but I didn't, and I regret this even today.

There was also a strange child named Wolfe, who in a none-too-subtle red light for OCD, would always receive the termly prize for tidying up the common areas.

Parents or guardians were nowhere to be seen and were possibly even deceased. During the school holidays Wolfe would remain with the headmaster's family while we eagerly made our escape in various family saloons along the rhododendron lined driveway.

Car marques and the relative attractiveness of each boy's mother were hot topics of conversation back in the dorm giving us an early taste of status envy. Pity the poor parent who had the audacity to park up in a battered old Hillman Minx.

The success of the system that kept us in check, therefore, relied heavily on there being limited cultural and social incursions into our rarefied, pared down world.

Unfortunately, my curiosity about life beyond the school grounds did eventually get the better of me. Striding out one break time over the nine-hole golf course in our camel-coloured duffle coats, my friend Atkinson and I cut through the rhododendron bushes by the lake. Beyond that lay some thick surrounding woodland and then, we presumed, freedom.

"Listen," said Atkinson, as our boots crunched on the dry twigs below. "I can hear a car. We can't be far from the road now."

"Yeah, let's try and hitch a lift to somewhere," I suggested. "Someone is bound to be going our way."

I could make out a perimeter fence in the distance. A bit more of a climb through the woods and we would be unstoppable.

"Oi, you two!"

It was Barry the new grounds man accompanied by some men and women in gumboots carrying shotguns. Real live shotguns with long shiny barrels. They were moving steadily forward about 200 yards in the clearing below us.

"Let's leg it!" urged Atkinson, tugging at the sleeve of my duffle coat.

"No, I don't think that's a good idea," I replied. "Look, can't you see that they're fully armed!"

I hadn't seen much of Barry before, only glimpses of him on his tractor as he manfully mowed the sports field or singlehandedly dismantled goal posts accompanied by a feisty looking Border Collie. I felt powerless as the rugged grounds man approached.

"Right you buggers, you're coming with me!"

Up close Barry was terrifying with his matted swept back Hell's Angels hair and strong tattooed forearms. A canvas bag slung over his powerful shoulders bulged with the bodies of some lifeless rabbits.

As the shooting party eyed us unsympathetically, Barry led us back down past the lake and over the golf course's fairway and eventually to the door of the headmaster's study.

"What the ruddy hell were you thinking of, going out of bounds?" said the exasperated head once we were safely inside his study.

"Don't know, sir," we replied in unison.

"Do you realise just how dangerous that was? The two of you could have been shot! How do you suppose I'd be able explain that to your parents?"

"Sorry, sir."

From where I was standing in his study, I spied two long thin objects protruding from a worn leather umbrella stand. One of the sticks was pale and perfunctory, the sort of thing you might use to clear some thick brambles in the back garden with. The other was fashioned from darker, more mature wood and had a curly handle and brass inlays. So which one was it going to be?

"Bend over, boy!"

I dutifully waited for the crack. Six of them in total, delivered by the master's firm and steady hand.

Having heard numerous tales about getting 'six of the best', including the one where you had to drop your trousers completely, I had finally experienced it myself.

Afterwards the headmaster held out his hand and I shook it, thinking all the while how little the punishment actually hurt. To the contrary, I felt elated it was all over.

"There," he said, closing the study door behind me. "Don't you ever do that again!"

By the time I had reached my classroom where a French lesson with Miss Jacques was in mid flow, it became impossible to ignore the burning sensation on my buttocks and across the upper part of my legs. I felt sick deep in my stomach and had difficulty in sitting down. Later in the communal showers, boys and staff alike winced at the sight of my bruised and blooded flesh.

Over the course of a few days the clear red stroke marks soon turned to purple and then horrific deep black stripes emerged over piss yellow streaks, which denoted the slowly healing bruises. It made my poor bum look like a Jackson Pollock canvas during the peak of American Expressionism. It took up to three months before the physical traces of my wounds disappeared completely.*

Around the time I was able to sit relatively comfortably again, we had an impromptu visit from a gang of skinheads from Crawley. This once small market town was one of the designated New Towns built to accommodate the overspill of working-class families from London who required housing after the war. The nearby diggers and cranes were an indicator that Crawley New Town was getting closer.

As we gathered up the leather footballs following one of Mr Arnold's rigorous Colts training sessions, this alarming group of lads in their long coats and buffed up leather boots loitered menacingly just a few yards away in the fog.

"Any of you lot want bovver?" shouted the tallest of the gang in his smart sheepskin coat.

"Ha, ha, ha! Betcha don't fancy a rumble," added a crop haired accomplice shaking a clenched fist at us.

Fraser, who had been playing in goal, must have been thinking quickly on his feet.

"Send for Slumbers!" he cried.

Slumbers was the biggest and quite possibly the toughest boy in the school, which wasn't saying much. On the other hand, he had by far the deepest voice of any other boy and wasn't far off from shaving. Yeah, Slumbers would tell them where to go.

As soon as Slumbers received the news, he manfully headed off in the direction of our exotic looking visitors. Fortunately, for him by the time he got there the skinheads had already slinked off.

Such encounters with the real world were the exception, not the norm. And for me, it took a major flu epidemic during the last throes

---

*Following a ruling by the European Court of Human Rights, corporal punishment by bamboo canes, slippers, 12-inch rulers and board dusters, was outlawed in Britain in 1986.

of 1975's long winter to find an answer to the school's incessant cultural stranglehold.

It was one of those rare situations where the sick outnumbered the healthy and, by day, the dormitories became more populous than the classrooms. The absence of the usual order of things and the staff members to enforce it (many were presumably struck down by a similar strain of the virus themselves) allowed time to stand still briefly.

And in this quiet unregulated utopia, akin to a safer and somewhat less fractious version of the *Lord of The Flies*, new friendships were forged and fresh, non-curricular ideas expressed as the days dragged by.

I made friends with a boy called Elliot, who I had never actually spoken to before. He seemed to find the then current Wall's sausages slogan 'Stab one tonight' particularly amusing. "Stab one tonight!" he would repeat deliriously before collapsing back into a deep sleep.

Someone had left a portable Roberts radio in the sick bay I had been dispatched to, from which emitted the latest chart hits on repeat; *How Long* by Ace, *Sing Baby Sing* by The Stylistics and *Whispering Grass* by Don Estelle and Windsor Davies from the popular television sitcom *It Ain't Half Hot, Mum*. Novelty records like *Whispering Grass* were a curse on the music charts of the mid-1970s. If it wasn't CW McCall and his big dumb trucks in *Convoy, The Streak*, a shameless cash-in on the fad for spontaneous nudity, would get you. Don't get me started on the insufferable romantic monologue *If* by Telly Savalas who, when not bothering the ladies with his cringe-inducing poetry, played the lollipop-toting cop *Kojak*.

Meanwhile, a week-old copy of the *Daily Mail* which had been going around the beds included a report on London club land's latest craze: the 1940s, inspired by the popular re-release of the wartime swing classic *In The Mood* by Glenn Miller.

Not that this was remotely in our thoughts, but such a creative and ideological lull in the entertainment world no doubt hastened the arrival of punk and the spiky declaration of 'year zero' just a couple of years later. As we sipped bitty watered-down squash to the sound of country and western, soft rock and Philadelphia soul, at least the brash and vulgar world of 1975 with its long hair (even our useless national football team had succumbed to the trend) and horrid Trade Unions was finding a way into this last post of Empire with its unapologetic house names Clive, Drake, Haig and Scott.

Despite there being a rather impressive oak-panelled library in the school, contemporary reading material was about as limited as the tactical skills of a certain World War One general my own house was named after.

One day our eagle-eyed choir master, Mr Schaeffer, caught me in possession of a rather racy paperback about sex and relationships. It had been passed on to me by Slumbers who looked about fifteen and had a Black Sabbath cassette tape hidden under his horsehair mattress.

"Is this your book?"

"No, sir, it isn't."

"Then, for goodness's sake, who does it belong to?"

"I don't really know, sir. I don't know what it's doing in my desk."

Fearing that he might report me to the headmaster and, who knows, another meeting with the dreaded contents of his umbrella stand, I was somewhat relieved to learn about the choir master's unusual solution to my alleged offence.

"So, you're interested in sex, are you?" asked Mr Schaeffer, getting me into a quiet corner of the staff common room.

"No, not really, sir."

"Now come along, Synge, every boy wants to know about the birds and the bees."

"Oh."

"Very well. I'm going to take this little book of yours away, and you're going to write me a very informative essay indeed telling me everything you have learnt about the facts of life."

"The facts of life?" I gulped.

"Yes, I want you to find out how people, ahem, 'do it'; you know, how men and women make little babies. You can research it all in the library. I'm sure you'll do a most excellent job."

Contrary to what Mr Schaeffer had suggested, few of the books available on the library's shelves were likely to assist me with such a daunting project. There were collected editions of Shakespeare, Dickens and Thackeray and some leather-bound volumes of

Country Life magazine, but none of these would provide me with the information I needed to complete the task. In the end, I found a few paragraphs about animal reproduction from the pages of *Encyclopedia Britannica*. Applying some of this knowledge to the most basic physiology of human beings, I then fleshed out a page of largely incoherent text. Well, what did I know?

> *'A reasonable enough try, but you don't include <u>nearly</u> enough detail on the precise act of love. At least you gave my wife and I something to laugh about!'*

So read Mr Schaeffer's feedback after I had handed back my findings to the required deadline.

I have no idea what this oddball would have made of some of the other books that found their way into my work desk. The well-thumbed paperback *Liquidate Paris* by Sven Hassel had been circulating among some of the older boys and, for a while, was secreted below my copy of *Civis Romanus*, the go-to Latin textbook of the day.

A favourite among impressionable pre-pubescent youths, Hassel's oeuvre stood out for their gory covers that depicted desperate, battle-scarred Wehrmacht troops stuck in various Eastern Front hell holes. With titles such as *Blitzfreeze* and *Legion of the Damned* they delivered when it came to sex and swearing, but in literary terms they ranked even lower than the dubious hack writing of Richard Allen's *Hell's Angels* and *Skinhead* books published by New English Library.*

More appropriate for boys my age, the headmaster would repeatedly point out, were the novels of Dick Francis, *The Hobbit* by JRR Tolkien or those rollicking adventure stories by Alistair Maclean, Captain WE Johns and CS Forester, author of the *Hornblower* series.

---

*Richard Allen was the pseudonym of Canadian born pulp writer James Moffat. He is thought to have penned almost 300 novels under 45 different aliases. His most famous works are the 'youthsploitation' novels which include *Skinhead* (1970), *Suedehead* (1971) and *Boot Boys* (1972).

It was a surprise, therefore, to find, in amongst a pile of battered Famous Five and Billy Bunter hardbacks lying around that somnolent sickbay, a book that I can honestly say, at the grand old age of eleven, was the first I had read enthusiastically from cover to cover.

'Jim Maclaine is a product of the fifties, when boys were spotty and girls were out of reach and nobody could play rock music like the Americans...'

So ran the blurb on the inside cover of the paperback *That'll Be The Day* by Ray Connolly. It wasn't long before I was hooked by this coming-of-age tale about the troubled and rebellious grammar schoolboy Jim (played by the dreamy looking pop star David Essex in the eponymous 1973 movie) who eschews the academic life for all the fun of the fair and other deadbeat pastimes in a gritty post-war seaside town.

At only 127 pages long, it could hardly be compared to the more literary minded *Journey's End* or *Great Expectations*, yet something about the story's themes of identity, escape and early sexual awakenings must have chimed loudly inside my pre-teen brain.

And after four years stuck in this Victorian-style fiefdom ruled by reactionary despots and opportunistic sadists, I began to wish I was more like the cruel and impulsive Jim.

Okay, so this misogynistic Jack the Lad was hardly what you would call an adequate role model for a future young gentleman like me, and his unsporting behaviour towards the ladies did leave a lot to be desired. But through the plain-speaking narrative and the tight, Hemingway-esque prose of author Connolly, himself an *Evening Standard* columnist turned screenwriter, the seedy world of fairgrounds, coffee bars and holiday camps opened my eyes to a fascinating milieu of low lives and the dead beats. How refreshing also to discover my first literary anti-hero, a type I would meet later in *Catcher In The Rye*, in the Ripley novels of Patricia Highsmith or via the short stories of Gogol, Dostoevsky and De Maupassant. Nasty Jim was way more compelling than the Empire-building bores and wood-dwelling wizards my classmates seemed so in awe of.

So with *That'll Be The Day* by my bedside, I tuned out from my stale and unhealthy surroundings for a few precious hours to follow Jim Maclaine as he bunked off school to taste real freedom, trading responsibility and later fatherhood for the lifestyle of a wild and itinerant rock and roller.

Up until this moment, I had struggled to get to the heart of most long-form texts I had been handed, but here the pages just seemed to turn themselves. All too quickly I reached chapter thirteen, the one in which Jim bumps into the archetypal rebel Johnny Swinburn and his band mates before agreeing to check out their show at the Floral Hall:

> *'Up there on stage, with their amplifiers turned full on, and their leather jackets shining in the lights they looked and sounded like stars. They were good and Johnny knew it.'*

Well, I thought. This life of popping coins in jukeboxes and sipping Cokes with girls called Shirley or Wendy sounds like a lot of fun. No wonder Jim wants to be more like his friend Johnny. Johnny was well on his way to 'making it', whatever that was.

As befits a story which strays into the dour 'kitchen sink' realism of *A Kind of Loving* or *Look Back In Anger*, the book ends on a sour note. Barely out of his teens himself, Jim leaves his young family, just as his own errant father had done before.

> *'By the bus station in town there was a music shop. I knew exactly what I must have…'*

Bad boy Jim ends up buying a second-hand guitar from the shop with his last remaining change, a scene which set up *That'll Be The Day's* film sequel *Stardust*, very nicely indeed.

'Remember the 60's?' was the question posed by the film's poster on its much-heralded release in October 1974. It featured a large photo of heart-throb David Essex holding a mean-looking bass guitar. A gaggle of adoring teenage fans reached out to him from below as if he were some kind of prophet. 'Show me a boy who never wanted to be a rock star and I'll show you a liar', ran another tagline.

Did I remember the 60's? Well, not exactly, but please do fill me in was my immediate thought.

4.

DEVIL GATE DRIVE

"Why didn't you go to the party?"

"Because, well…because there's a tiger there."

"*What* did you say?"

"A real tiger, it's there in that house!"

"Oh, don't be so silly!"

"I saw it with my own eyes, mummy. It was lying on the floor staring right back at me. It was HORRIBLE!"

"Never mind, darling. Daddy will take you back to the party. Everything will be just fine."

Escaping from the jaws of a Bengal tiger in Morden Road was just one of the hazards of growing up in South East London in the late-1960s.

The occasion was a birthday party for a boy from my nursery school called Ben. All of four years old, I was feeling terribly grown up as I walked unaccompanied the few blocks to the address a little bit further on from Pond Road and the church.

In one hand I carried Ben's present, a Shado 2 mobile half tacker with rocket launcher from the Gerry Anderson series *UFO*. In the other, a signed card depicting a smiling elephant wishing him a 'Big Happy Birthday'.

The beautifully boxed vehicle was chosen specially from a selection at Raggedy Anne's, the toy shop in the village run by Mr McKenzie, who with his bald shiny pate looked remarkably like Yul Brynner in the film *The King and I*. With its floor to ceiling Hot Wheels cars and accessories, its mouthwatering range of cowboy clobber and glistening new bicycles at the back, I could have spent hours in his shop. The half tracker was perfect, said my mum as we took it to the till.

Turning left at the red post box just as mum had told me, I arrived at the house, a handsome half-timbered 1930s semi. Unable to reach the buzzer high up to the right of the door, I put down the freshly wrapped parcel and the card. I had to use both hands to force open the letter box.

"Hello? Is anyone there?"

And there it was. A monstrous snarling skull with thick dark stripes crisscrossing its broad circumference and, a little further forward, gaping jaws revealing two gleaming white canines just ready to sink into their prey.

Thwack!

I let the heavy letter box go.

Panting heavily, I back pedalled down the terracotta steps to consider my next move.

Er…run for it!

Music, art and book lovers themselves, mum and dad met while both studying at Trinity College, Dublin, in the 1950s. Dad was a former wartime evacuee and Englishman abroad with literary aspirations and a famous ancestor, the Dublin-born playwright John Millington Synge, author of *The Playboy of the Western World*.*

Mum was the bright and beautiful dark-haired Ulster girl who would bid farewell to provincial Ballymena in County Antrim for a new life in England.

*Synge's play provoked riots when it opened at the Abbey Theatre, Dublin in 1907. A Sinn Féin leader called it "a vile and inhuman story told in the foulest language we have ever listened to from a public platform".

Dad was an instinctively creative and fun-loving person and, despite his solid background, had a rebellious and mischievous streak. He liked pubs and painting water colours *alfresco*, loved the sun and sea swimming and, with his novelist hat on, always seemed to have the plots of far-fetched adventure stories whirling around his curious and original mind. His language was playful and rarely too sincere or boring, He had special names for people which often belied their true character; the pub for instance was 'Jolly John's', our short-lived Friday cleaner 'Cheery Mary' and the curtain twitching neighbours were 'The Fun Gang'.

Mum was elegant, poised and just a little measured. Some would have mistaken this last trait for stand-offish-ness but she just liked things to be a certain way, whether it was the use of language, the position of a living room chair or the ingredients or texture of a home-made Spanish omelette. She hated swimming and didn't care much for the sun. Growing up in Northern Ireland her devout mother told her that it was possible even to drown in a puddle.

After national service and university, dad initially found work as an advertising copywriter with the firm Ogilvy & Mather. Looking to start a family, the young couple settled in Blackheath, with mum trying her best to return to glory our rather ramshackle Georgian home, which had wobbly floorboards, steep wooden staircases and a long thin garden that backed onto some newly built Span houses.*

When visiting, on one occasion, my aunt claimed she had felt a strong spiritual presence by the garden door. The toilet (or 'loo' as mum insisted it was called) to the right of this spooky corner had a 150-year-old ceramic cistern mounted on the wall with a worn wooden antique seat to match.

In contrast to our characterful yet unwieldy dwelling with its old brass beds and dark antique chests, the neighbouring Span homes were distinguished by their cool open plan interiors with floor-to-ceiling windows guided by the architectural principles of the Bauhaus movement.

*Span Developments were the brainchild of modernist architects Eric Lyons and Geoffrey Townsend who built over 2,000 homes in southeast England during the 1950s and 1960s, notably in Blackheath and in New Ash Green, Kent.

Even at a very young age, it seemed to me as if the world was divided into those who clung to the past, like my parents with their heavy bookshelves and traditional heirlooms, and those more forward thinking-types who embraced modern gadgets, colour televisions and brutalist glass and concrete.

Mum, who busied herself with the shopping and the cooking and the occasional bout of China mending or private French tuition, attracted a parade of local acolytes drawn from all classes and generations.

In an early line up was a bulbous-nosed female painter who drove a battered old Morgan sports car and a lady we called 'Auntie Marie', whose henpecked husband, Joe, gave us extra Maths tuition. Poor Joe must have waited hours outside our house while his wife – rarely pausing for breath – went into one of her epic monologues in a piercing Welsh Valleys accent.

My mum and the childless Auntie Marie didn't seem to have a lot in common other than a shared interest in charitable causes – the saving of the green belt, the British Legion's annual Poppy Day appeal and a children's care home in nearby Abbey Wood, among others.

Mr Williams, who had a small grocery business in nearby Lewisham, was another regular. With his little van, his pencil and notepad at the ready and a permanently furrowed brow, he would wait patiently at the doorstep for my mum to relay her order to him. "Some eggs, let me see, maybe a bit of cheese…"

Again, the social transaction seemed to take an age and I wondered whether my mother's in-built indecisiveness was the reason behind this. Whether mum's vagueness was some kind of affectation or not, I decided there and then I would be super decisive myself with clear plans and opinions, no matter how unpopular they may be.

"Mum," I piped up from my position next to her fashionable Scholl sandals, "can we please have some chocolate Nesquik?"

Like his arch-rivals in the local grocery business Cullen's, Mr Williams would eventually close his shop following the arrival of the more affordable and infinitely better stocked Safeway supermarket at the newly built Riverdale Shopping Centre.

Modelled on a typical US shopping mall, the centre boasted an ingenious musical clock comprising of several animated figurines based on typical south London types: the tailor, the Pearly Queen, the fishmonger and the naughty schoolgirl. Each would appear on the hour drawing crowds of onlookers in the process. Mr Williams was undoubtedly a Lewisham type too, but never made it as a character in this proud civic display.

Walk on parts in my mother's domestic idyll went to a number of other characters who, in their own small way, influenced this child who strayed none too far from his mother's skirt hem.

Lynn, a classic 1960s dolly bird with a short mini dress and heavy mod eyeliner, took me out in the pram and would do bed and bathtime duties on my mum's night off.

Mrs Fitzgerald, who had recently retired from her job running the local post office and was looking for a less challenging part-time job, came in on Fridays to do the hoovering. Before that, we had a cleaner called Mrs Ruddock, a severe looking German lady from Ladywell whose husband Albert was a Desert Rat and had seen action at El Alamein.

Dad's friends came from a world far beyond suburban Blackheath and tended to be literary collaborators drawn from the creative departments of London's in-demand advertising agencies. Fruity voiced ad man John stayed late for whisky-soaked writing sessions (under the pseudonym Christopher Leopold, John and my dad published a quartet of pulp-ish thrillers) while a softly spoken graphic designer named Norman accompanied dad on work trips to Northern Ireland and the Low Countries. A few, like the eccentric poet and writer Marvin, were discovered in Soho pubs after office hours.

"Hey, Danny," he would say to me during one of his unannounced visits, "I hear you're gonna bowl at me, right? Oh boy, how I love to smash your bowling, ah ha, ha-ha-ha-ha!"

Brooklyn born Marvin, who lived in New York but spent just about every summer on the London literary scene, was in love with baseball as well as the sound of his own booming voice. Every time Marvin stayed over, my friends and I were summoned to bowl over after over at him on the rough grassy heath. Still dressed in his shabby black suit and sporting a behind-the-ear hearing aid, he swung his big bat around like Mickey Mantle, the New York Yankees legend.

"Ah huh, huh, huh, huh, huh…" he would grunt excitedly as the hard leather ball sailed repeatedly into the main road.

"Oh boy, do I like cruggit!"

Big Marv also adored my mum's cooking and, returning from our sweaty evening workout, would singlehandedly devour one of her home-made shepherd's pies.

Dad enjoyed turning the most unlikely people onto our summer game. Indeed, he liked doing this so much he compiled a series of essays on the subject: *Strangers' Gallery: Some Foreign Views of English Cricket*. He even wrote to the great Groucho Marx* asking him to submit a chapter but instead received a signed publicity photograph with this most succinct of messages: 'I don't know balls about cricket.' Dad framed the photo and hung it on the wall directly behind his writing desk.

Nestled in a vale tucked behind acres of flat common ground crossed by the busy A2 towards Kent, Blackheath Village was just about the perfect place to start a young family.

Although small children like us often attracted disapproving scowls from members of the older generation who walked by the house, including one severe-looking lady in mourning we named 'Queen Victoria', this Narnia-meets-Nutwood of uncongested streets and modernist cul-de-sacs offered us both safe spaces and the relatively wild and free. And if, like me, you owned a bicycle with stabilisers the kingdom was practically yours.

Primary school started at the age of four. Our education was yet to become demanding or regimented and we filled our days pretending to be Batman and Robin or watched the caterpillars we had caught in the bushes turn into majestic butterflies.

The dinner ladies had nothing on mum's cooking (she had worked as an *au pair* in France and could do Elizabeth David's repertoire**

*The moustachioed Marx brother experienced an afternoon at Lords Cricket Ground in 1954. "What a wonderful cure for insomnia," he surmised, "If you can't sleep here, you really need an analyst."

**Cookery writer and author of *A Book of Mediterranean Food* (1950).

standing on her head) and the pink semolina was to be avoided at all costs. That didn't stop us from breaking into rowdy choruses of *Back Home* in the lunch queue as World Cup fever hit Manor Park Primary during the summer of 1970.

Back home they'll be thinking about us
When we are far away
Back home they'll be really behind us
In every game we play

In their plain crew-necked white or red shirts and no-nonsense, workaday haircuts, Hurst, Moore, Charlton and Banks were names to be reckoned with. Their faces were chiselled onto silver coins that we collected from the petrol station.

Trying to emulate Pele and his teammates from Brazil – "And it's four!" went the Kenneth Wolstenholme commentary after Carlos Alberto's rocket finally sunk the Italians – we fell over clumsily like the stag beetles we teased on the way home. Luckily a nurse was on hand to apply industrial sized helpings of TCP to our grazed knees and elbows.

At least we didn't end up like that hapless burglar (actually a copper in disguise) who helped take part in an educational visit by the local police. While the entire school looked on in horror, the poor man ran the length of the sports field before an enormous Alsatian dog was unleashed, leaping up to grab the man's right arm and pinning him violently to the ground where he lay motionless for a few seconds.

We applauded nervously when he rose from this most unpromising of positions, coming over to us immediately with flecks of grass on his jumper and a heavily bandaged right arm.

Years later I wondered whether this show of power was an attempt to attract future recruits. Or perhaps it was simply their way of telling us that crime doesn't pay. I certainly developed the habit of avoiding large dogs from this point on.

In Blackheath we were also fortunate enough to have interesting and ever-so-slightly bohemian neighbours. Among them were architects, painters, illustrators, fine art lecturers and a strikingly tall shipping broker from Holland. And, as if by some divine order, they all seemed to have children my age.

Michael, who lived just three doors down would walk to school with me in his green snorkel parka. His parents both collected and made modern art and in their spare time listened to old jazz and blues records. They named their cat Kenneth Clarke, after the art historian and presenter of the ground-breaking television series *Civilisation*.

Their kitchen/diner smelt of garlic and refried kidney beans and they served up things my mum didn't, like huge mugs of Bovril and roughly cut slices of toast and Marmite from a traditional brown Hovis loaf.

Michael had three much older sisters who wore kaftan coats and swore like troopers. His dad always seemed to be in his workshop which was in the basement. He stuffed his pipe full of Ready Rubbed and was always mending things, unlike my own dad who smoked filtered cigarettes and spent his spare time writing ad copy or speculative works of fiction on a clunky old typewriter.

The sound of handheld drills, revving lawnmower engines and crackling bonfires were a sure sign that the male householder was around. In our house, the constant hammering on the Olivetti's keyboard was the accompaniment to our south London Shangri-La. *Tap, tap-tap, tap-tap-tap, tap, tap, tap-tap, tap, tap* … echoed through floorboards as we drifted off to sleep each night.

Michael's dad was practically bald, drove an orange VW camper van and wore a plain navy Guernsey sweater, even in the summer. Mine had thick curly hair, wore a dark suit and knitted tie and commuted daily to an office in the West End.

But occasionally my dad would pull a big surprise out of the bag, such as the shiny maroon Wolseley Six that appeared on the road one evening outside our house.

"Right everybody, we're going for a drive," he announced. Then all of us – Nathaniel our old roué of a tomcat included – piled into the back of this extraordinary executive vehicle with its walnut dashboard and sumptuous leather rear bench for a spin. "Is this going to be our car?" we pleaded as we cruised along the empty roads that crisscrossed the dark expanse of the heath. The driver could barely wipe the smile off his face.

Sadly, this was the last we were to see of the Wolseley. It turned out to be a vehicle on loan from a client at my dad's advertising agency. For reasons such as this, Michael and I could never truly agree on whose dad was the best.

In our road, a gang of boys soon formed over various garden fences. Along the old boundary wall at the back, we would meet up to plan our own brand of suburban mayhem, dressed in our arty middle-class uniform of flared corduroy jeans and woolen jumpers that our mums had knitted for us. Dan, Michael, Nick and Simon. For a fleeting moment in our lives, we were the fab four.

Such was the bravura of this gang and its hangers on from the nearby estates that we would break into abandoned villas, roam the local allotment with its graffitied old pillbox or pick fights with anyone foolish enough to stand in our way. Adults were nowhere to be seen.

On the walk back from school one afternoon, I wrestled a turf rival in nearby Kidbrooke to the ground only to realise halfway through our tussle the poor kid was supported by one tin leg. I stopped the fight immediately when this became apparent, after which I gave him some of my bubble gum. He then calmly rolled up a billowing trouser leg to show me the sorry-looking stump that was encased inside.

Incidents like these only help to illustrate the near total absence of health and safety in our 1970's childhoods. Being a simple car passenger, for instance, was akin to joining a round of Russian roulette in downtown Hanoi. There was no legal reason to wear a seatbelt* and the laws regarding smoking and drinking were far less punitive, with speed limits there to be broken in the absence of speed cameras or efficient traffic calming measures.

I had previously suffered a split lip and a cracked tooth after Mrs McLean (Michael's mother who would die of cancer only a few years later) had to slam on her brakes while on school pick-up duty. And by the age of eight I had inhaled several packets of cigarettes thanks to my dad's nicotine habit.

---

*Safety belts didn't become a legal requirement for drivers until 1983.

My younger brother, whose tiny infant fingers I had once accidentally shut tight inside our rear passenger door, used to moan about how long car journeys made him feel sick. The cause of his complaint? A combination of warm plastic and poly fabric seats along with Elgar, Bruckner and other such stirring classical music coming from the car radio. Could it have also been the cloud of nauseating black smoke being blown back into his face as one of dad's Rothmans smouldered on the in-car ashtray?

"Look, I don't need to wear a seatbelt," dad would maintain, as he illustrated his own personal safety manoeuvre in the event of a collision: two hands placed firmly on the steering wheel at ten to two.

There were risks even when you were in positions of relative safety. For instance, when I was seven, I set off on a solo visit to Grannie Jean, my Northern Irish grandmother who lived in a tiny old cottage overlooking the Malvern Hills in deepest Herefordshire.

This entailed my mother putting me on a train at Paddington while she asked a total stranger sitting in the passenger compartment with me to make sure I changed trains at Evesham. The outbound journey went off without incident, but the return leg was different.

My aunt, who lived near my grannie and was a country GP, had arranged for me to return as a passenger on a working ambulance that so happened to be travelling to London.

This time I was handed over to a couple of drivers who must have been in their late twenties accompanied by a more mature looking nurse. They seemed like an experienced and responsible bunch. What could possibly go wrong?

Indeed, everything appeared to be going to plan as the vehicle rattled along the dark country lanes of the north Cotswolds and then the newly built M40, me fully strapped down in the patient's cot with the veteran nurse sitting comfortingly by my side.

I must have dozed off completely when, suddenly, there was the unnerving sensation that we were spinning out of control and then everything came to an abrupt stop. It was pitch black and it felt like I had been pinned violently to the side of a wall.

I had experienced something similar before. Dad had once taken us to the Wall of Death at the decrepit Festival of Britain fun fair at

Battersea Park. Backing up nervously against the wall's giant cylinder, which made a dreadful screeching noise as it revolved, I screamed out loud as the floor disappeared beneath me.

Anyway, the next thing I knew I was being hauled out through the back doors of the stricken ambulance which was now lying on its side somewhere along the Goldhawk Road. There was smashed glass everywhere. As a crowd of people stood and stared, an unknown Good Samaritan figure whisked me up and, still covered in my grey hospital blanket, I was placed in the back seat of a police car which then sped me all the way to Blackheath, arriving sometime after midnight.

I was sufficiently wide awake to notice the two on duty officers settling down to drink some Scotch with my dad. After enjoying my dad's hospitality, the heroes in their smart blue uniforms disappeared back into the night in their powerful Rover saloon.

One gloomy Saturday afternoon towards the fag end of 1973, my dad inexplicably got into the habit of taking me and my older sister, Sam, to our nearest record shop.

"Choose one single each," were his magic words.

After rocking up to Nicholl's, the hi-fi and audio repair specialists on the Lee High Road, we trooped up to the doorway where, pasted inside the glass window, was a list of the week's best-selling singles.

"Ooh yes! I want the new one from David Essex," Sam exclaimed as she stuck her forefinger over *Lamplight*, which was a new entry at number 38.

Having to go on tiptoes to read the top of the list, my eyes hovered over the very latest entries, stayers and fallers.

I had already heard the instrumental *Eye Level* by The Simon Park Orchestra on the Motorola in dad's Triumph and Alvin Stardust's new one *My Coo-Ca-Choo* was also a contender for my 50p piece. With his big sideburns and black leather catsuit, Stardust had been on *Top of the Pops* only the week before.

"What about Mud's *Dyna-Mite*... or, erm *Photograph* by Ringo Starr?"

"Get Mud!" urged Sam.

"Barry Blue?" I thought out aloud. "Do you think that'll be any good?"

"Ringo," countered dad. "After all, you like The Beatles, don't you?"

"Yeah, The Beatles are the best."

Inside the shop was a mouthwatering selection of new hi-fi systems and radios with some wire record racks and a few plastic-lined LP carry boxes lining the floor. In a corner, a tall wooden cabinet displayed, in strict alphabetical order, a selection of albums.

"Can I help?" said the shop manager, who wore a suit and tie much like Brian Epstein had done in the NEMS record shop in Liverpool.

"Yes," said dad. "We'd like *Lamplight* by David Essex and the boy wants *Photograph* which I believe is number 13 in the charts. Isn't that right, Dan?"

I nodded, glad that Ringo's latest release would shortly be in my hands yet cringing at the sheer embarrassment of the scenario. You see, record shops, or at least the trendier chains such as Harlequin or Virgin, were hardly angling for the custom of us pre-teens accompanied by our awkward Hush Puppy-wearing fathers.

Such establishments were staffed not by polite middle-aged men in plain thin ties but by the local tank topped or cheesecloth clad Buddhas of Suburbia. These jumped-up shop assistants were simply desperate to recreate a Chelsea Drugstore vibe from the film *A Clockwork Orange*, in particular the scene where the high-minded Alex peruses a Top Ten that includes Heaven Seventeen and Johnny Zhivago.

And in contrast to the unchallenging easy listening tones of Mantovani or John Denver available at Nicholl's, their in-house musical choices would come blasting through speakers which looked like they belonged to Hawkwind's road crew. Loud Mick Ronson-ish guitar riffs or harsh slap back vocals – the kind heard on John Lennon's *Cold Turkey* or *Money* by Pink Floyd – was a none-too-subtle cue for mum and dad and their smaller charges to step outside.

Returning home with my purchase, I was immediately drawn to the stunning photo of the bearded drummer, singer and now film director covered almost head to toe in silver foil.

I played it a few times on the family record player and it had a familiar and reassuring sound to it. With the ex-Beatle I was undoubtedly in safe hands, but was Ringo's songwriting ability really on a par with Lennon and McCartney's? Even I could tell that *Photograph* was hardly the sonic snapshot of '73.

So, the next time we all went shopping for singles at Nicholl's, I decided to take a chance. My second choice turned out to be a real belter, an eventual number one no less.

Getting this item home, I immediately sampled the heady joy of removing the record from its crisp paper sleeve. I was dazzled by the sheen of the vinyl which appeared as black and as shiny as a fresh oil slick. Holding this artefact up to the light, I could only stare in wonder at the tall clipper boat framed by a calm blue sky on the label's inner circle. It put me in mind of the Kon-Tiki from Thor Heyerdahl's extraordinary voyage across the Pacific Ocean – another book on my school's approved reading list. Three bold capital letters printed in dark blue around the mast area was a reminder this was a RAK Records production.

RAK was the then recently formed label owned by producer Mickie Most aided by the song writing team of Nicky Chinn and Mike Chapman. Collectively dubbed 'Chinnichap', they went on to pen a sequence of number one hits for groups such as Mud, The Sweet, Racey and Hot Chocolate.

RAK's signature sound was pounding repetitive drums and double tracked guitars with catchy football terrace-friendly choruses enhanced by shouting, whistling and other excitable crowd noises. Their early to mid-1970s output came as close to the brief as possible for rock and roll's original remit, as described by George Melly in *Revolt Into Style*: 'a contemporary incitement to mindless fucking and arbitrary vandalism: screw and smash music'.

'Hey, y'all wanna go down to Devil Gate Drive?'

A coarse and shouty female voice implored as the needle hit the record's groove.

'Yeah!'

The reply sounded like it was coming from a gathering of the sort of teenagers my mother might have disapproved of. Thudding reverberating glam rock drums then took over, which had the effect of sending my pulse rate soaring and my young head spinning wildly.

I began to wonder where all this was taking me exactly.

'Welcome to the dive.'

Another voice, this time male with the tone and timbre of a slightly menacing fairground worker calling out the last ride at the dodgems. What on earth was a *dive*, I wondered. Was this somewhere I really wanted to go? Too late. The shriller, more excitable female voice was now counting the song in:

'Er one, er two, er one two three…'

The singer is Suzi Quatro, a 24-year-old bassist from Detroit, Michigan, who had been flown across the pond by hotshot producer Mickie Most, already famous for producing hits for The Animals and Herman's Hermits.

On a business trip to the Motown offices in downtown Detroit, the cigar-chomping impresario spotted her performing at a local gig with her all-girl band Cradle and had the good sense to offer her a deal on the spot.

Midas Most, who while on the popular television talent show *New Faces* earned himself a reputation as a harsh critic of aspiring new performers, was quick to transform Suzi's image from happy-go-lucky hippie chick to out-and-out ballin' rock queen.

Encased in a tight zip-up leather jumpsuit which was accessorised by various chains and chokers, she was later seen on *Top of the Pops* prowling the stage wielding an enormous white Fender Precision bass. At least it looked enormous in the photo from my sister's *Jackie* magazine; Quatro is only five foot two inches tall.

To the hard rocking twelve-bar boogie, Suzi then led a resounding call to arms aimed, it would seem, at pre-teens exactly like me. At nine or ten years old you are already beginning to exercise your hard-wired sense of nostalgia. You are already mourning your lost innocence:

Well at the age of five they can do their jive
Down in Devil Gate Drive
And at the age of six they're gonna get their kicks
Down in Devil Gate Drive

What the hell! Everything I had heard up to this point was manna from heaven to this shy, pre-pubescent boy and as every essential 3 minutes and 57 seconds of this 45-rpm disc kept playing, I found myself delving deeper into Suzi Q's universe.

I decided there and then that Suzi was my perfect pin up poster girl. With her pouting, strutting stage presence, twinned with her obvious musical prowess, she was like your coolest older sister. She was a genuine American too, raised in a solid Detroit working-class neighbourhood and descended from Italian and Hungarian immigrants. Not like those Limey imposters who shared the chart run down with her; Mud, Alvin Stardust and The Rubettes. No, Suzi was the real deal.

As the record kept revolving, she then dealt with the more serious stuff; the mental and physiological changes that older teens must go through during puberty. To my ten-year-old ears it didn't exactly sound like plain sailing:

When they reach fifteen, that's when they all get mean
Down in Devil Gate Drive
When I was sweet sixteen, I was the jukebox queen
Down in Devil Gate Drive

The last line was accompanied by a very crude male wolf whistle. Clearly, it wasn't just *me* who thought this singer was a bit of alright.

By now, fully immersed in Suzi's rock and roll boogie-woogie party, I detected a distinctly sexually charged atmosphere. To me, this was a new and slightly dangerous feeling. In fact, such was the record's erotic undertone that I decided I would definitely not play this in the shared company of grown-ups.

Later, after lights out, I would furtively kiss her cute face which peeped out of a dyed feather cut bob sourced from a page in *Jackie*.

Put it this way, I wasn't going to bop up and down to this in front of Grannie Squirrel, like I had done previously with *The Laughing Gnome* or *Crocodile Rock*.

Now, as the jet-black disc began to run out of grooves, Suzi rallied her all-male band of Brit-born session rockers together for one crazy, climactic finale. She is the real boss now, albeit a slightly kinky looking one in her thigh length platform boots and head-to-toe leathers:

'Come on boys, let's do it one more time for Suzi! Are you ready now?

'Yeah!'

By the time the record climaxed on one sustained guitar chord, aided and abetted by the drummer's flailing toms and cymbals, I could only reel back exhausted from this rush of pre-teen adrenaline mixed with a powerful hint of testosterone.

I felt sweaty and slightly used but decided immediately to return the needle to the start.

Hey Suzi, can we do this all over again?

5.

WHITE HEAT

That Suzi Q totally rocked my world and, in the process, changed my psyche forever, is beyond doubt. And as when the boy puppet Pinocchio ran away from Geppetto to join the wayward children on Pleasure Island, *Devil Gate Drive* suggested an alternative route to becoming a 'real boy'*. It was a road that seemed noticeably free of books, timetables, responsible adults and enforced 'good behaviour'. I liked it but feared it in equal measures.

But would my parents have noticed a clear behavioural pattern emerging here? After all, in the short ten years of my life my passions had segued quickly on from kittens and cowboys through to Action Man, The Beatles and now glam rock, or at least the poppier, more commercial end of it. Where would this all end?

I had grown up wanting to be Doug McLure in *The Virginian* or Pete Duel in *Alias Smith and Jones*, gashing my leg horribly on an old wooden sawhorse in the back garden which had rusty nails sticking out of it.

Strange as it may seem, we simply could not get away from the great myths of the Wild West. Quite remarkable, considering cowboys

*"**How do you ever expect to be a real boy?**" asks **Jiminy Cricket** in **Walt Disney's** *Pinocchio* **(1940).**

had died out around the year 1895 and, besides, were really only active for a period of 30 years. On our black and white television set during the school holidays, there were endless reruns of *The Lone Ranger, Rawhide* and *Champion The Wonder Horse*. My parents too had raved about a new film they had seen at the Lewisham Odeon, *Butch Cassidy and the Sundance Kid*. Dad even grew his sideburns out like Robert Redford's handsome, happy-go-lucky outlaw. In the so-called swinging decade, the names Wyatt Earp, Daniel Boone and George Custer meant more to me than The Monkees or Davy, Dozy, Beaky, Mick and Tich.

When, mistaking it for a horse, I swung my unfortunate leg over that lethal work bench, I was wearing my mum's suede waistcoat with a tin sheriff's badge pinned to its top button hole. On my head was a homemade Davy Crockett raccoon hat while stuffed into the waistband of my Wrangler blue jeans was a replica Colt 45 revolver that fired reel after reel of single shot caps. I was a real smokin' gun.

Like so many middle-class households, we began to reap the benefits of scientific innovation and economic advancement; the 'White Heat of Technology' as Harold Wilson coined his famous 1963 speech to Labour delegates. First came the rectangular modern fridge freezer, then the automatic washing machine and, finally, the big family colour television set which arrived just in time for the 1972 Olympic Games held in Munich. My parents could hardly be accused of being early adopters.

Indeed, only a few years earlier we had struggled to spot men walking on the moon via a tiny black and white Sony portable. Now, here was Mark Spitz in star spangled Speedos and little Olga Korbut pirouetting across a disturbingly iridescent gymnasium floor.

From cowboys I gravitated to a more contemporary embodiment of masculinity, Action Man. Yet another find from the well-stocked shelves of Raggedy Anne's, my first action figure (definitely not a doll, as some might have cleverly surmised) was a blonde-haired, square jawed squaddie I named Peter Loggs. I carefully wrote his name down in pencil on the accompanying plastic dog tag.

Initially his wardrobe was a little threadbare; the basic action figure came with a standard facial scar and plain olive-green garb. But, as I began to acquire more outfits for him, he showed a remarkable and quite treacherous ability to change sides, masquerading as both a ruddy mariner and polo-necked French Resistance fighter then defecting to the Germans and back again as a World War Two Russian infantryman.

Action Man's manufacturers were wise to Peter Loggs's ever shifting allegiances and created a system in which he might feasibly enjoy a supply of new uniforms for life.

A trio of bright red stars appeared on the packaging for each new product which I enthusiastically cut out and glued onto the front of my personal Action Man Star Card. Having accumulated 21 of these stars, I would then send by post the completed Star Card to the manufacturers Palitoy of Coalville in Leicestershire. As if by magic, a new buck-naked action figure would arrive in a plain cardboard box in just a matter of weeks.

With such an ingenious consumer cycle in place, was it any wonder that Peter was soon joined by a suave brown-haired trooper I named Rodney Wade and later, Alex, an enigmatic infantryman distinguished by his missing-in-action surname and fuzzy blonde 'realistic hair', an innovation that Palitoy launched in 1970?

Of course, while my men were busily reenacting Stalingrad or the breakout at The Bulge, I was coming to terms with the fact that my own place in the family hierarchy was coming under repeated attack.

I had been wildly enthusiastic about the arrival of my baby brother, who I immediately fancied as a new playmate; someone I could hand my holster down to, a deputy who could mind the fort as I roamed the plains around SE3 on my Raleigh Rodeo. But the sad truth was he wouldn't be straying much further than mum's carry cot. At least for the time being.

If, in Beatles terms, I was a straightforward 'Yes please Mister Martin' *Beatles For Sale* or *A Hard Day's Night* kind of baby, Miles was almost certainly a child of the band's later experimental period. Born in the era of 'free love' and growing civil and political unrest, he would almost certainly be aligned to the more fluid doctrine of *The White Album* and *Abbey Road*.

Like in one of those stoner-ish psychedelic party scenes from a 1960s counterculture movie, time would stand still for him and his sweet mother (my mother!) as I went about doing normal boy stuff: school, friends, bike rides and episodes of *Doctor Who*.

Now with a domineering pre-pubescent older sister and a needy baby brother a good five years younger than me, I therefore had no choice but to become the middle one.

John F Kennedy, Martin Luther King Jr and Michael Jackson were all middle children, so I was in good company, but with my mother now doting on flower child Miles, it looked suspiciously as if I had been left out in the cold.

It was around this stage that John, Paul, George and Ringo came to my aid. Their earliest Parlophone singles were already ingrained during infancy, my sticky wet fingers reaching for *Day Tripper* or the underrated *You Can't Do That* whenever I needed a quick fix of raw Beatles power.

As a five-year-old, I would stack these and other 45-rpm discs, several of them at a time, on the record player's spindle. I cranked the lever to automatic mode then watched as each one plonked down like a rescue dinghy from some kind of groovy technicolour Sea King helicopter. The end of Sandie Shaw's *Tell The Boys* would cue up *Granny* by Cat Stevens followed by The Move's *Blackberry Way* and so on, ensuring that, in our house at least, the 1960s never really ended.

In tune with the times, my sister Sam boasted a wardrobe that consisted of heart shaped clogs, a mirrored velvet waistcoat and a feather boa sourced from shopping trips to the 'with it' Kensington emporium Biba with my stylish mum.

Mum was so particular about clothes that we would travel all the way to Islington just to buy our jeans. These weren't just any jeans, but fine brushed cotton or bold denim and corduroy ones in an assortment of different styles and colours.

With such attention to detail, I could have passed as a miniaturised member of one of those late-1960s boy bands in my rounded-collared paisley shirt, brushed cotton Levi's bell bottoms worn with a white leather belt and suede Clark's desert boots.

Dad, who must have been quietly disapproving, eventually came around to The Beatles after they released the concept album *Sgt. Pepper*, making a copy of it on his old reel to reel tape machine by placing a

Grundig microphone to the record player's pathetic mono speaker. This method would hardly have impressed readers of *Hi-Fi Weekly*.

By the time I had begun to take them seriously, the fab four had gone their separate ways and were each pursuing solo careers. I knew this because it said so in my prized copy of *The Beatles Story, a Story of Pop Special*.

According to this beautifully put together colour magazine, the once cheeky Merseyside mop-tops were now four rather serious individuals: John, a 'Man Who Cares', 'Wing Commander' Paul, 'Mystic Maestro' George and Ringo? Well, he was simply 'Ringo'.

But even in the revised cultural landscape of 1974, there must have been some hope of a reunion. Late-to-the-party types like me desperately scanned the weekly schedules in *The Radio Times* for a showing of *Help!* or *A Hard Day's Night*.

For at least three Christmases running my parents gifted me albums from the back catalogue. One magical year my festive haul included *Rubber Soul* and *Revolver* with the bonus of Alan Aldridge's *Beatles Illustrated Lyrics Vol.2*, a book that interpreted the Lennon and McCartney oeuvre with some unsettling Pop Art surrealism. I think I preferred the artwork on the albums.

In reality, the age of prog, glam and hard rock signalled hard times indeed for Beatles fans. For a start, we had to make do with pale imitations such as Badfinger and ELO.

Then came The Rutles, a comic send-up of the fab four which was first aired on *Rutland Weekend Television* created by ex-Bonzo Dog Doo-Dah Band member Neil Innes and Eric Idle from Monty Python's Flying Circus.

The later Rutles film *All You Need Is Cash* had reassuringly familiar set pieces (The Cavern Club, Shea Stadium and the legendary Savile Row rooftop show) plus some artful pastiche songs – *I Must Be In Love* and *Cheese And Onions* being the stand out tracks – yet earnest young fans like myself detected a cynical note to the venture.

Why was the late Brian Epstein now being referred to as 'Leggy Mountbatten'? It seemed disrespectful. And why did Mick Jagger feature so heavily in a long and very boring mock interview?

To be fair, the four ex-band members hadn't exactly set the world alight with their solo projects. I loved *Band On The Run,* but both Paul and George's albums were hit and miss affairs. Ringo Starr's directorial debut *Born To Boogie* sounded good on paper but the live footage of Marc Bolan needed a more meticulous edit and the druggy outtakes ("some people like to rock…some people like to roll…") simply weren't funny, unless you were stoned yourself, which of course I wasn't.

And having promoted peace and 'bagism' and then settled into Manhattan's Upper West Side with Yoko, John was having his infamous 'lost weekend' with wild Harry Nilsson and Yoko's assistant May Pang before going on to record the underwhelming Phil Spector-produced covers album *Rock 'N' Roll* in 1975.

Fortunately, I had by now managed to snare at least half of their albums. More significantly, I had regular access to Michael's copy of *The Beatles 1962-1966.*

Known as 'the red one', it was a whopping great double sided gatefold LP with hits from the early Beatlemania days to their glorious middle period – *Girl, Paperback Writer, Eleanor Rigby* – plus the one we music-hacks-in-waiting would mercilessly lift the needle for: *Yellow Submarine.*

My love of the band didn't go as far as growing my hair out like John's or adopting the dry Scouse drawl of George but, at one stage, there was a plan for Michael and I to raise enough money to buy a second-hand Hofner 'Beatle bass', the one played by Paul McCartney even today, which we had seen advertised in a tobacconist's window. At the princely sum of £15 this was of course out of the question, so grabbing a few cardboard boxes and some grey and black poster paint his art lecturer dad lent us, we settled instead for making a couple of air guitars. Once our instruments were ready, we performed mime versions of *Come Together* and *Get Back* to just about anyone who was prepared to listen; Grannie Squirrel, Mrs Fitzgerald the cleaner, and even Michael's sniggering older sisters.

Undaunted by the fact there was, as yet, no George or Ringo, Michael confidently air strummed his John Lennon Rickenbacker copy while I held up my still drying Gretsch Countryman (actually one of George's guitars) leaning into my dad's Grundig microphone for the *shum-dum-diddely-dums.*

Even without a proper band or indeed any real instruments, it was possible for my friends and I to engage meaningfully with the music we had been turned onto. The Canadian cultural theorist Marshall McLuhan must have had exactly our type of behaviour in mind when he coined his mantra 'the medium is the message'.

McLuhan conceived and then ran amok on US television chat shows with the idea that the nature or form of the medium (such as the television set or the radio), was more significant than the meaning or content of the message (the programme that was being watched or listened to).

His own pithy soundbites about the electronic age in which he lived through, 'hot' and 'cold' media, 'the global village' and others, are often misinterpreted today.

Put simply, McLuhan's 'medium is the message' recognises the moment when audiences – whether sitting in front of a television set, next to a radio or recording their favourite new tracks with a portable cassette player – begin to actively engage with the medium thereby creating their own meaning through it.

McLuhan observed that while the age of the printing press had made everybody a reader, the invention of the Xerox copier had made everybody a publisher. Essentially McLuhan foresaw our behaviour in the era of the Internet, particularly regarding social media use, content sharing and digital streaming platforms.

Armed with a home-made cardboard guitar and my sister's portable Sony cassette player, I knew zilch about McLuhan's theories, but quickly proved the medium was indeed the message by recording my own personal chart run downs using mostly Beatles records and speaking in phoney American DJ-ese. Unwittingly, I was becoming a content creator.

Running out of records to play, I would then record short sequences from *Top of the Pops,* placing the recorder's in-built microphone as close to the television set as possible. From this popular weekly show, only a handful of songs would make it onto my final edit. The light-hearted banter from studio presenters like Dave Lee Travis or Noel Edmonds had to go of course, often mid-sentence. It was hardly the most technically accomplished version of a modern playlist, but at least it was mine. I had engaged actively with the medium.

Another skill needed to produce this decidedly analogue version of Spotify was making sure that during a performance by, say, Pilot or Cozy Powell, an adult or sibling didn't burst into the living room while you were in the middle of recording.

Cries of "Has anyone seen my Spirograph pens?" or "Can't we turn over for the end of the cricket?" would spell disaster for any carefully curated edit.

What I had gleaned from reading up about The Beatles or watching endless weekly transmissions of *Top of the Pops* was that rock stars inhabited an entirely different universe from ours, or at least seemed to.

Unlike mortals such as Michael and myself, they were completely unbounded by class, gender, race or, in the case of David Bowie miming along to *Starman* on the telly, sexuality.

It was as if they had some special power, a power that only seemed to increase with the outrageous costumes or outlandish modes of behaviour they adopted. Rock stars seemed to exist purely for the glare of the studio lights, their hysterical teenage fans or the clicking of a camera shutter.

Now, thought this curious and creative middle child from the dawn of the beat era who had had his fill of cowboys and Action Man, and instead had dozens of catchy melodies swirling around his little head. Wouldn't it be a good idea to be just a little bit more like them?

6.

MIRROR STAR

"Dan!"

I was buzzing around the bedroom pretending that my dad's old squash racket was a Fender Precision bass guitar. For authenticity's sake, I had even attached a length of thin rope around the head that ended at the floor-to-ceiling Habitat shelving unit where my record player was installed.

I'm a member of the band Penetration and we're halfway through the pop/punk anthem *Come Into The Open*. You know, the bit where the song breaks down for a few bars then builds up again before crashing back into the rousing chorus sung by punk poster girl Pauline Murray:

Come into the open
There's nothing left to hide
Come into the open
Where I can see your face among the crowd

"Dan, Dan!"
A more insistent knock this time.
"Wot is it?"
How I wished the nagging voice from the hallway would go away.

I just had to keep on going until the start of that killer bass run, the one that herald's the song's devastating finale.

My dad again.

"Come down for supper, for heaven's sake. We've been calling you for hours!"

In the summer of 1977, my unimaginative and somewhat retrospective taste in music (Beatles, Stones, Motown etc.) was challenged when Hari arrived for a play date.

Hari was a local boy I had known since nursery and had previously joined me in ruff tuff war games as well as outings to Greenwich Park on home-made skateboards.

Hari wore his straight jet-black hair well below the ears and had a huge gap between his upper two front teeth. He adored nature and in his bedroom was an alarming stuffed barn owl and an illuminated glass tank, inside of which he kept a tropical spider. Hari claimed this beast was a tarantula just to scare everyone.

During a car trip to the south coast to see his grannie, we had sung along heartily to his cassette tape featuring the rock and roll hits of Chuck Berry, Jerry Lee Lewis, Eddie Cochrane and others. Dropped in the centre of Brighton by his mum, we took ourselves off to an afternoon showing of *The Spy Who Loved Me* then mooched about the amusement arcades, before getting the bus back to his grannie's village in the South Downs. Whether it was skateboards, music, Bond cars or exotic pets, Hari was always into something new.

When I opened the front door, I could tell that something about him had changed. For a start, the free-flowing hair that had made him look like an Apache warrior had gone, replaced by a short and spiky number.

He wore a studded leather wristband on one arm and his plain black drainpipes had zips and safety pins running along their seams. A complicated series of straps and buckles joined his legs together. Under another arm he clutched some LP's and a handful of 7-inch singles.

"Baby, baby, baby!" he began singing as we headed upstairs to my bedroom where my record player was.

"What's *that*?" I asked, thinking this was all a little strange.

"It's the new Vibrators single. Look!"

He handed me one of the singles which I examined for further clues to its identity. Sure enough, the song was *Baby Baby*, by a band called The Vibrators.

"I bought this the other day Danny (nobody else called me Danny!), but then realised my sister already had a copy. You can have it for 50p. Thirty if you take this one as well."

He passed me another single, this time by a band called The Jam who, like Hari, had short spiky hair and looked rather cross and moody.

I suddenly felt a little self-conscious in my mud brown corduroys and sensible Clarks walking shoes. Perhaps this visit by Hari was a forewarning that something seismic was coming my way.

"Okay, I don't know about The Jam but I'll take The Vibrators. Erm, are you *sure* it's any good?"

Hari nodded.

Hmm, I thought, he's been put up to this by his older sister, the one with the Lou Reed *Transformer* poster on her bedroom wall. The one who was always having dreadful shouting matches with her mum. Hari didn't even like *Baby Baby. Baby Baby* was a dud, a reject, a proper stinker. It also had a small crack on its outer groove. But maybe I needed to give it a few plays before I could deliver a proper verdict.

Later that summer, I had something of a masterclass on new bands with my older cousin, Philip. On his tinny bedroom record player he played me selected tracks from albums by Dr Feelgood and Eddie and the Hot Rods, which I liked a lot. *Down By The Jetty*, in particular, stood out for its gritty, almost primeval sound. Indeed, the raw unfiltered racket of the Feelgoods made his Stones album sound like The Dooleys or Captain & Tennille.

"Play that one *Roxette* again, Phil. I've never heard anything quite like that before."

Then, after making sure the bedroom door was shut tightly, Philip cued up the Sex Pistols track *Bodies* from the album *Never Mind The*

Bollocks. It was about a girl from Birmingham called Pauline who 'lived in a tree' and had suffered a terrible abortion. The angry wall of guitars hit me right between the eyes and threatened to drown out the whiny singing which, with the use of some choice swear words, suggested some extremely unsavoury images indeed. It was hard to know what to say after hearing that.

Cousin Philip had his naughty rebellious side, but he wasn't what you would call a punk rocker – how could you, being an athletics and football nut living in the wilds of Herefordshire? He was a Manchester United obsessive who, when not booting a ball backwards and forwards in his parents' yard, would sprint up and down the lane holding a big red plastic stopwatch my dad gave to him as a birthday present.

If anything, Philip was like the character in the song *My Perfect Cousin* by The Undertones; smarter and sportier than I was with a knack of beating me at Subbuteo and table tennis. But he did know somebody who *was* a proper punk.

Just a little further down his lane in a pronounced dip in the valley was a tiny, converted garage where Mark lived.

Following the acrimonious departure of Johnny Rotten, Mark had been one of those teenage hopefuls to audition for the role of lead singer of the Sex Pistols. My cousin claimed he was going to appear in a new film called *The Great Rock 'n' Roll Swindle*.

"'Ello mate, you alright?" said a lanky ginger haired lad in a fluffy red mohair jumper, greeting us at the door of his lair.

Offering us each a mug of tea, Mark promptly placed the latest Generation X album on an altogether more serious looking turntable. Philip told me that Mark had his own band and drove all the gear to gigs in an old postal van. How cool was that? Only a year earlier we were playing football with this boy and his chubby younger brother in their back garden.

"'Ave a listen to this," he said, placing the needle into the groove of track number two.

First came a dirty repetitive guitar riff. Then a sharp but tinny drum roll. We were in! In almost perfect unison the three of us began nodding our heads, chewing our own imaginary stick of gum in time with the music. The track was so fast our necks could barely keep up with the pace.

A hundred punks run with London town
Down Wardour Street to the Soho Sound
Don't sleep all week only when they fall down

The singer was Billy Idol, the good-looking guy with the spiky blond crop and comic book sneer who sang *Ready Steady Go* on *Top of the Pops*. But this tune *One Hundred Punks* was better. It felt more authentic. It was more heartfelt and convincing. Even in this cramped man cave, it made me want to get up and pogo. I really wanted to rumble with Billy's sussed-up Soho crowd. And, if Mark had asked right there and then, I would have gladly signed up with his band of bumpkin punks too.

Only a year earlier I had left boarding school after one final run in with Pig Nut. The embittered old matron had singlehandedly ruined my post-confirmation treat – a delicious fried scampi platter with my parents in a Brighton restaurant – by shining a torch directly into my face at two in the morning.

"How *dare* you wake everyone up by coming in late!" she hissed, jabbing me repeatedly with her fore finger. "You ought to be ashamed of yourself!"

The effect of the naked torchlight against her blubbery porcine features was terrifying. So alarming in fact that the next day I wrote a very distraught letter to my parents telling them in no uncertain terms that I had had my fill.

The message must have finally driven home and shortly afterwards I was enrolling in an all-boy's institution located on the fringes of South East London where inter-war suburbia meets rural Kent. My new classmates were now the scions of chartered accountants, solicitors, teachers, car dealers and master butchers.

Ties were slackened, H's were dropped and each day began with a bus ride to the gates where swarms of sweaty but soberly clad pupils rushed in for morning assembly carrying a variety of multi-coloured Adidas sports hold-all's. Oh, so many Adidas hold all's.

I knew almost immediately that my sober black briefcase with its brass clasp and corners had to go.

During the lunch break we played endless games of football on the hard concrete outside, arriving even sweatier to our afternoon classes. Prepubescent body odour was an occupational hazard.

My own was offset somewhat by lashings of Brut 33 shampoo, a sporty, manly scent endorsed on the telly by the boxer Henry Cooper who had famously floored the great Cassius Clay with a brutal left hook.

Unfortunately, the distinctive 'Great Smell of Brut' was too much for some of the passengers on the bus ride home, especially when my hair got a good soaking in the rain.

"Who's wearing that yucky aftershave?" said one older schoolgirl, who I quite fancied, as she looked over to the rear seats where I was cowering. I went bright red and sunk even further into my seat. Henry and his mate Kevin Keegan, the permed golden boy of English football who also appeared in the ads, had a lot to answer for.

Mum and dad had, in the meantime, moved from Blackheath to a house in Greenwich, just the other side of the heath. The family home they had spent so much time, money and energy doing up became a treacherous and watery wreck after our washing machine span out of control spurting gallons of soapy hot water through the very core of the 150-year-old building.

As everybody was out for the day, we could do nothing to stop this disaster. I guess mum and dad simply couldn't face starting out all over again so, instead of fixing the place up, they started to look elsewhere.

Shortly after we settled into the new house, our little road held a street party for the Queen's Silver Jubilee. There were children's relay races, cans of Party Seven bitter for the grown-ups and a huge bonfire that fizzed and crackled into the night, thanks largely to the efforts of a retired local policeman who doused the flames with the contents of an old jerry can.

Only a few miles away on the River Thames, the new *enfant terribles* of pop, the Sex Pistols, played an impromptu live concert from a hired riverboat that sailed to the very heart of the establishment. Had Westminster's MP's been sitting, their anti-social message would have been heard loud and clear in the galleries of the House of Commons.

The band's manager, Malcolm McLaren, had gambled that the publicity stunt would provide valuable column inches in his quest to get his ill-behaved charges to number one with their alternative national anthem *God Save The Queen*. It did, but for his trouble, the police roughed him up and arrested him, along with 11 other partygoers. The Sex Pistols are notorious for many reasons, but this summer river excursion was a defining moment in their all too brief career. In the week of the Silver Jubilee celebrations, Rod Stewart hit the top spot with the ballad *I Don't Want To Talk About It*,* but it was the Pistols who won the front page headlines setting the template for every future rock and roll media caper.

Stately Greenwich and its declining industrial neighbour, Deptford, were remarkably close to Blackheath yet seemed miles apart both culturally and socially. In Greenwich, a largely derelict-looking seamen's hospital that squared up to the Thames was the centrepiece around which a circuitous high street accommodated antiques and second-hand book shops, working caffs and a fair few pubs, named mostly after famous admirals or sea going vessels. An 'astonishing cartouche sandwiched between power stations' opined the renowned architectural critic Ian Nairn.**

There was undoubtedly a rough and ready charm to the place. Here among the bricks, the buddleia and the neo-Classical rubble off Burney Street, we unearthed tin helmets, naval ratings' smocks and elegant Art Deco soda syphons at the weekly flea market.

My parents knew men with long beards and paint-splattered cable knit jumpers who did up tall Georgian or Victorian town houses

---

*Despite bans by the BBC and major retailers such as WHSmith and Woolworths, *God Save The Queen* reached number two in June 1977.

**Nairn's London*, 1966.

which would be worth over £1 million in 30 or 40 years' time. One of these was a part-time actor who did a neat line in cheap salvage items, stripping old pine furniture and timber floors on the side.

A taste for Victoriana among the middle classes was picking up after years in the style wilderness. While landlords and homeowners had once unceremoniously torn out original cast iron fireplaces with their surrounding William Morris ceramic tiles, such items, alongside coal burners, natural pine dining tables, illustrated prints, lampshades and even chamber pots, penny-farthing bicycles and stuffed animals had become *de rigueur* again.

Even in dour mid-1970s Britain, people like my parents and their friends could enjoy the semblance of an intellectual life with plays at the rebuilt theatre in Crooms Hill (legendary music hall artist Max Wall brought the house down with *The Entertainer* in 1974) and what might have been the country's first ever wine bar, the pretentiously named Bar du Musée on Nelson Road, where the trucks and lorries thundered past on their way to the industrial wastelands further east.

A long straight foot tunnel, accessed via an old service lift next to the imperious tea clipper, the Cutty Sark ('one of the fastest ships of its day'), led to the Isle of Dogs on the opposite side of the river.

We used to race from one side to another on our bicycles howling all the way through to maximise the effect of the reverberating acoustics. Or maybe because secretly we imagined that one of the supporting cast iron walls would suddenly give way, leaving us only seconds to exit the ice-cold watery chasm.

Emerging safely on the north bank, we would treat ourselves to a Strawberry Mivvi from the kiosk on Island Gardens and then almost immediately turn back. Nothing of interest lay beyond this quiet, uneventful corner except some abandoned warehouses, a few idle cranes and pockets of humble terraced housing – the last remnants of a truly working-class neighbourhood that could be traced to the time of Dickens and beyond.

As if our family wasn't already large enough now that all three children were living at home, my mother – who at heart was a caring and charitable Christian – rented out the spare bedroom to paying lodgers and, at times, anyone who needed a safe haven in times of distress.

There was the pretty Australian Goldsmiths College student with the boring computer scientist boyfriend and then a quiet academic who worked two days a week at the National Maritime Museum. Before that, while I was away at school, there was the troubled young boy with an unfortunate pudding bowl haircut called Sebastian. He was the son of my dad's work colleague, who the courts had decided was unable to live with his own mother. She, after all, had been accused of her husband's murder in a suspicious house fire and was awaiting trial. Until the fraught custody battle was resolved, Sebastian would be staying under my parents' roof.

Understandably, the poor fellow was sensitive and moody and prone to terrible outbursts of rage, during which he would shriek like a Banshee and throw his, and very often my, toys around.

He absolutely destroyed my painstakingly put together scale model diorama, which featured an Afrika Korps Kubelwagen and a motorcycle and sidecar painted in realistic desert brown. The RAF could not have done a better job.

For some strange reason the soundtrack to the musical *The Rocky Horror Picture Show* seemed to calm Sebastian down and so it played in our house incessantly.

To me there was something highly objectionable about Richard O'Brien's camp, sci-fi romp – even *before* I saw the film – but such a lovely smile came over the young lad's face during songs like *Science Fiction*, *Dammit Janet* and the *Time Warp* that you simply wouldn't dream of taking the needle off the record. And if you had, he would have screamed the bloody house down. Nobody wanted that.

Retreating to my bedroom, which was now adorned with *Sounds* and *NME* covers plus a giant colour photo of Blondie's singer Debbie Harry Blu Tacked above my bed, the inevitable drip, drip of punk rock began to have an effect.

I ditched my Adidas t-shirt, the Gola trainers and the Falmer 'Country Cousins' flared jeans and gave myself a disastrous self-inflicted punk rock haircut. The crude handiwork with mum's scissors had to be rectified almost immediately by an alarming-looking number one at the local barber's. With this shocking new look, I could have passed for one of those Crawley skinheads who had made such an impression on me all those years earlier.

Further emboldened, I raided Sam's record collection and, tucking a few LP's under my arm, took *Brain Salad Surgery* by Emerson Lake & Palmer and Deep Purple's *Made In Japan* to a second-hand record shop on the High Road, trading them in for some cash which I spent on singles by Rich Kids and The Skids. From humble beginnings starting with the admittedly not-very-punk *Like Clockwork* by The Boomtown Rats, my singles collection was really starting to take shape.

Thanks also to a tip off from Hari, whose school mates The Screaming Midgets were down to be the support act, I also experienced my first rock concert, The Fabulous Poodles at the Albany Empire in Deptford.

Trying to look my very punky best in shiny brown DM's and a fluffy V-neck jumper worn without a shirt, me and my latest school friend, Alex, accompanied by his kid brother, Miguel, wandered along Deptford High Street looking for the venue.

It was dusk and the shops already had their shutters down. We were well and truly lost and there simply wasn't anyone around we could ask.

Then, all of a sudden, a battered looking white Mini Clubman came screeching along the high street. Bizarrely it headed directly towards us then braked violently as it mounted the pavement.

I could see four or five of them squeezed into the vehicle. There was music blaring out from some in-car speakers and the spiky haired driver took swigs from a bottle of Merrydown cider.

"'Scuse me," said the young man in the passenger seat after winding his window down, "but does anyone know where the frigging Albany is?"

"Nah, 'fraid not," said Alex, "we're lost ourselves."

The boy giggled.

"Oh, never mind. Er, by the way, we're the Screaming Midgets, why don't you lot come and see us play tonight? We'll be on at about eight o'clock."

"Yeah," slurred a voice coming from the fug of cigarette smoke in the back, "you could be our roadies."

Cue more guffaws from the back.

"Tell the geezer at the door 'We're with The Fabulous Poodles' and they'll let you in for nuffink. 'We're with The Fabulous Poodles', got it?"

Wow! we all thought, as the Midget-mobile sped off in the direction of Creek Road. The Screaming Midgets have asked us personally to their concert and we were going be their roadies. We must be proper punks, or at least we must *look* like proper punks.

Once inside the venue, the words "We're with The Fabulous Poodles" having failed to work their magic on the doorman, we began to soak up the intoxicating sights, sounds and smells of our very first 'gig'.

None of us smoked, drank or did drugs. Having been turned away previously for being two- or three-years underage outside a Lurkers concert at Thames Polytechnic in Woolwich, we were just grateful to be allowed in.

In fact, it was exciting enough just to squat there together in the aisle marvelling at all the equipment on stage and tapping our feet to the crackly old ska music that thudded out from the in-house PA system.

The support acts, The Screaming Midgets and The Red Lights, who had some punk cred for appearing on a *Live At The Roxy* compilation album, were okay but, in our opinion, not quite up there with Squeeze or Subway Sect, who were clearly influences.

The headliners, meanwhile, were not what we were expecting at all. The lead singer wore geeky glasses with roundish red frames and a shiny blue suit. He looked really old and had a sort of Buddy Holly thing going on with his Stratocaster and oversized glasses combo. His sidekick at the front of the stage wore a bow tie and played mostly the violin in between bouts of singing. With his slick dark hair and thin pencil moustache, he looked uncannily like the matinee idol Clark Gable. But boy, they really could play.

Every song the singer introduced seemed to have a strange title that went straight over our underdeveloped brains; *Anna Rexia, Pink City Twist* and the indecipherable *Rum Baba Boogie* among others. In the mould of Elvis Costello and the Attractions and Joe Jackson, The Fabulous Poodles were basically a tight rock and roll outfit, albeit with mysteriously arch lyrics delivered by your coolest Humanities lecturer at college.

We didn't exactly rush out and buy their latest album *Think Pink* (nor it would seem did the record buying public) but their show did leave our ears ringing for days afterwards.

Their song *Mirror Star*, which failed to even reach the Top 50 in 1979, seemed to sum up my then state of mind perfectly.

> *Head's in the clouds on school reports*
> *He's always lost in other thoughts*
> *Made no difference, shut them out*
> *He'd be a star someday, no doubt*

School was tolerable but I was becoming increasingly lost in a system which seemed to value only exceptional sporting or academic prowess. I sensed even more strongly there could be another world out there for people like me. Preferably one with bright studio lights, shiny new guitars and amplifiers, hot girlfriends – any girlfriend! The ones from the pages of my sister's *Cosmopolitan* magazine seemed nice – and a crowd that accepted me for who I was.

Now, if only I knew how to get there.

7.

THIS YEAR'S MODEL

Thanks largely to my chance encounter with The Fabulous Poodles (or the Fab Poos as those in the know called them), I found myself stuck in the headlights of a brand-new music movement: new wave. Now, here was a scene I could really get on board with.

Not to be confused with the influential French cinematic approach, new wave was a lazy moniker, coined presumably by someone at the *NME* for the kind of offbeat music that didn't quite match the requirements of the safety pins and anarchy brigade.

The sound and the look of new wave shone out from the crowd with its outrageous coloured vinyl pressings, skinny-tied band members, modish synth and organ motifs, and often crude allusions to 1960s pop and soul. In the hands of leading new wave artists like Elvis Costello and Talking Heads, songs were delivered in a nervy, hurried whine and spoke heavily of the suburban, white-collar experience and the ennui of an increasingly mechanised workplace. So sang *Martha and the Muffins* on their 1980 hit *Echo Beach*:

> *From nine to five, I have to spend my time at work*
> *My job is very boring, I'm an office clerk*
> *The only thing that helps me pass the time away*
> *Is knowing I'll be back at Echo Beach someday*

Closer to home, I was more than a little envious of Alex's copy of *The Sound of the Suburbs* by The Members which he had on clear vinyl. For me, the innovative artwork that appeared on the record sleeves and the full-page ads in *Sounds* and *NME* was all part of the appeal. I soon had an entire wall of these in my bedroom.

Must-have singles by the Buzzcocks, X-Ray Spex and Blondie were material embodiments of the day's infectious can-do, punk-lite attitude. Meanwhile, names like The Cure and The Vapors were dropped like cultural cluster bombs via tiny lapel pin badges that ended up on our school blazers. Collars up, of course. In the break, we read up on more underground acts in photocopied fanzines which we bought while waiting in the queue outside The Marquee or the 100 Club in Oxford Street. It felt like something was happening at last.

Not quite punk yet hardly the polished rock performers they must have secretly wanted to be, new wave artists shone briefly as the decade turned. But by 1980 the movement had fragmented into power pop, synth pop, goth and post-punk, a complex music genre best understood by listening to the Rough Trade sampler *C81*.

Launched in collaboration with the *NME* in May 1981, the cassette tape featured a roster of left field artists including Josef K, The Raincoats, Furious Pig and Cabaret Voltaire. It pointed to a thousand new musical directions that would eventually find their way into the 1980s mainstream.

My favourite was the tape's opener, *The "Sweetest Girl"* by the oddly named Scritti Politti. Expecting more edgy guitars and politicised soundbites, it was instead an understated lo-fi dub reggae groove that played on for a full five minutes with the occasional melodic steal from a post-Beatles George Harrison.

"This is bollocks!" I told Alex when I handed back the copy he had lent me. "It sounds like it was recorded in a Notting Hill squat."

And more than likely it was, but, by now, this eccentric tune with its intellectual hinterland signposted by Green Gartside's gorgeous male vocal had seeped into my consciousness. Just don't ask me what it all meant.

Back at school, I had been put in the bottom set for Maths with Mr Ramsay, a somewhat dry Welshman and hard taskmaster with a 'take no prisoners' approach to teaching his useless charges.

"This homework wasn't very good now, was it?" he chided me after a particularly sloppy attempt to convert a sheet of vulgar fractions.

"I mean, why didn't you ask me during the class if you didn't understand?"

"I made all the notes, sir, but when I got home it just didn't make a lot of sense to me."

"Oh dear, that is a shame," said Mr Ramsay. "How would you like to drive a white van then?"

"Sorry?"

"I mean to say, would you like to spend your future days at the wheel of a white Ford Transit van?"

"Erm, well, I've not really thought about it, sir."

"You know, one of those vans that you see driving up and down the high street. It sounds a lot of fun, doesn't it?"

"I wouldn't know, sir."

"I bet you could have a bloody whale of a time with your pals in one of those vans. You could lean out of the window and wave at all the pretty girls. You could listen to the radio all day long and stop somewhere pleasant for lunch. You could smoke endless cigarettes, tell dirty jokes and read your newspaper. You wouldn't need to answer to any boss or go into a stale, lifeless office or anything like that. You could just do your own thing while sitting up there in the van looking down on everyone else. Now, what do you reckon?"

"Well, I'm not..."

"It could be an absolute riot, couldn't it? But not, I'd imagine, for very long. I mean, has it crossed your mind that you might spend a considerable amount of time stuck in the most terrible traffic jams? Perhaps life driving a white van around London isn't all it's cracked up to be, after all."

"Er, well, maybe..."

"It would simply become so damn *boring*! So tedious in fact you might want to strangle the bloke sitting next to you. Have you thought about that? Not only would you be driven absolutely nuts by the endless traffic lights and the road signs and all those bloody speed bumps, but you might feasibly end up on a murder charge!"

Mr Ramsay handed my workbook back to me with its terse corrections in red biro.

"Now, *that* is why you need to pass your Maths O-Level."

We were fortunate that our liberal leaning English teacher, a Bob Dylan nerd in a brown corduroy suit, had, in his wisdom, helped to set up a Rock Society so that we could play our favourite music on a communal record player during the lunch break.

It was an inspired idea and popularly received by the pupils, yet this well-intentioned initiative merely helped to illuminate the clear cultural divisions present among this collection of boys aged roughly 14 to 18 years.

Basically, there were the older sixth formers with their army surplus greatcoats, long unkempt hair, facial 'bum fluff' and Hawkwind albums bulging out of plastic Virgin Records store bags. And us, the younger and (so we thought) more streetwise students armed with 7-inch singles by Generation X, The Ruts and Penetration.

It was war.

The long haired grebos didn't stand a chance as we hogged the single deck to the rabble-rousing sounds of *Tommy Gun* or *Into The Valley,* thereby condemning arguably more worthy albums by Van der Graaf Generator and The Alan Parsons Project to the metaphorical 'bargain bin'.

Of course, individuality wasn't easy to pull off in a sea of dark and sober school uniforms. Nevertheless, potential outsider types like us, who had already conceded some ground to the punk blitzkrieg, found a number of resourceful ways to adapt to the shifting world order.

Ties, which were previously worn like variations of the 'kipper' as modelled by Peter Wyngarde in television's *Jason King* or by Dennis Waterman in *The Sweeney*, suddenly got thinner and knottier. If you could hang a conker off it, you were on the right track. Raiding our fathers' wardrobes we plundered old black Macintoshes, M&S polo necks and skinny three-buttoned jackets.

In the playground, Dr Martens boots (DM's) began to replace the regulation black lace ups from K Shops or Freeman Hardy & Willis. And, if you were unfortunate enough to be lumbered with a pair of unfashionable black flares, you could always beg your mum to take them in.

Meanwhile, my plain cardboard ring binder ceased to be a mere repository for pages of notes and formally assessed essays. It now served as a blank canvas for the carefully hand-drawn band logos I perfected while the teacher was talking; The Specials, XTC, Spizzenergi, The Rezillos and my imaginary Swinging London-style psychedelic outfit The Mint Umbrella.

Gigs came and went: Protex at the London School of Economics, The Photos, The Ruts and Nine Below Zero at The Marquee, and then the first sighting of a little-known band from Manchester who supported my favourite band, the Buzzcocks, at The Rainbow.

Finsbury Park is a long way from South London but after just a few stops on the Victoria Line Alex and I found ourselves in the bustling Seven Sisters Road one drizzly November night.

The Rainbow had seen better days as the impressive 3,000-seater Astoria cinema but it still had an imposing Art Deco entrance. Its lobby area boasted a tiled Moorish-style fountain similar to the one in The Alhambra in Granada.

A crowd of young punks and older men with beards and long coats were either pressed against the bar or checking out the merch stall selling tour posters for the band's new album *A Different Kind of Tension*.

"Come on," I said, "let's check out Joy Division,"

"Yeah, don't wanna miss them," replied Alex.

It was almost pitch black in the vast auditorium but there was no seating, so we could choose just about any standpoint we fancied.

The four band members walked on stage and then plugged their instruments in without any fanfare; northern men with plain dark shirts, demob style trousers and short haircuts. Not your typical rock stars but, then again, the look was somehow fresh and ever-so-slightly subversive.

As Alex and I stood in this gathering of no more than fifty, it was clear even before the pale and stick thin singer began dancing in his idiosyncratic way, that they would be something of a game changer.

"That song *Dead Souls* is good."

"Yeah, too right!"

"D'you reckon they're gonna play *Transmission*?"

"Er, dunno."

"That's a brilliant song too."

"Yeah, fucking amazing!"

Standing mostly still and eschewing bright guitar chords and classic Beatle-y melodies for something darker and more minimal, Joy Division had a ready-made sound that totally transfixed me.

I had already bought their first single *Transmission* which John Peel had played on his late-night show on Radio 1. But here the dark intensity of the song was more palpable as Peter Hook's rough bass line echoed around the still largely empty space in front of the stage.

Taken alone, the words referred to a sort of strange live broadcast (*'Listen to the silence, let it ring on…'*) but, unable to put any tangible meaning together, I opted for the music. Joy Division had a visceral and unsettling quality but at times they conjured up moments of outstanding beauty. The enjoyment of live music, I was quickly grasping, was not necessarily about what you heard, but often what you *imagined* you heard.

The eccentric singer exhorted us several times to *'dance, dance, dance, dance, dance to the radio'* before he simply walked off. Most singers would wave as they left the stage. Ian Curtis looked as if he was going to fetch a biro or some paper clips from the office stock room, leaving the band to finish without him. After what seemed like an age, their set eventually came to a close. A solitary drummer played out his busy yet perfunctory beats while an abandoned guitar fed back through the PA. Then the lights cut out.

Now, if I had been Pete Shelley and Steve Diggle about to follow this up with songs from *A Different Kind of Tension*, I might have given up there and then.

I can't say that Curtis and Joy Division were entirely to blame, but at home I was increasingly moody and monosyllabic. My dad was constantly reminding me of the saying 'no man is an island'.

No man is an island, Entire of itself,
Every man is a piece of the continent,
A part of the main*

*From *Devotions upon Emergent Occasions* by John Donne, 1624.

At school I didn't seem to excel at anything on the curriculum It was frustrating to say the least. What's more, my newly found punk insouciance was getting me into trouble.

One afternoon I was sent to the Deputy Head, Mr Brand, to explain why I hadn't appeared for a detention.

"Come in. Ah yes…Synge. It's about the detention you missed last week."

I nodded.

"You did miss the detention, didn't you?" he asked, finding the notes in front of him.

"Yep."

"Very well, so you have a doctor's note with you. I simply need to make a record of it before I sign it off."

"No, I don't have a doctor's note."

"Sorry? So you don't have a reason for skipping the detention with Dr O'Hagan last Friday?"

"No."

He looked up from his papers and had a proper look at me this time. From my usual seat far from the stage in morning assembly, he looked like the sort of teacher that was best avoided. Too old. Too establishment by half. I don't think we had ever been in the same small room together until then.

"So," he continued calmly, "what *was* the reason you were unable to attend?"

I sighed.

He lit up an Embassy Mild and eased back slightly in his chair.

"There wasn't a particular reason, sir. I suppose I was just tired after a long day. I felt like I needed to go home and have a rest."

There was a much longer pause from Mr Brand this time as I could see his brain frantically computing itself for the necessary response. "You wanted to go home because you were *tired*?" he boomed, bringing down his fist on the desk in front of him.

"Well, yes, I suppose that's correct. I was tired and I'd had a particularly bad day."

Mr Brand didn't need to add anything else. His contorted beetroot coloured face and the shaking right hand that fumbled with the cigarette lighter on his desk said it all.

For my sins, I was handed an extra four weeks of detention as punishment.

I fully deserved it.

In truth, I was sleepwalking through secondary school. However hard I tried, I never seemed to impress my teachers enough. I desperately needed someone to step in and help give me the confidence boost I so badly needed. But that person never appeared.

Consequently, nothing seemed to matter more than this music. And like so many teenagers all over the land, punk's irresistible energy and lack of deference for what had gone before swept me up and encouraged me and a couple of similarly inclined classmates to form a band of our own. What did we have to lose after all?

Perhaps this explains why, as Jim Maclaine had done in the teen pulp classic *That'll Be The Day*, I found myself, aged just 15, standing outside a junk shop in Woolwich cradling a newly acquired second-hand electric guitar.

So far so good, but how on earth was I going to play the bugger?

8.

IMAGINARY BOYS

To the average person, a six-stringed electric guitar is just another musical instrument. They look quite cool, they're loud and have a distinctly rebellious image. Your mother wouldn't necessarily want you to bring one home.

For others, there are almost religious connotations to this mass-produced item. In the wrong hands it can make an ungodly racket but, in the right hands, it can turn you into a real god.

The first electric guitars appeared after some bright spark came up with the idea of attaching an electric pick up to a regular acoustic model. In pre-war swing and jazz bands the lone acoustic guitar was often drowned out in a sea of brass and percussion and so the innovation of this single pick up that sent signals to an amplifier helped push the humble guitarist towards the musical front line. But it wasn't until the 1950s that electric guitars really came of age.

Thanks largely to developments by Californian manufacturers Fender, with their mass- produced Telecaster and Stratocaster models, followed shortly by Gibson's iconic Les Paul, it became possible for those workaday strummers to move even closer towards the spotlight.

"It was like something from space," recalls Hank Marvin of The Shadows on seeing his first US-imported Fender Stratocaster or 'Strat'.

This sentiment certainly chimed with my own teenage self as I marvelled at rows of highly polished yet sadly unattainable Fender, Gibson, Rickenbacker and Gretsch models propped up in the window of Macari's music shop on the Charing Cross Road.

It's funny but, even today, there is something quite magical about the effect of some simple stage lighting on a cherry red or sunburst coloured hard bodied guitar.

Discovered in a Woolwich junk shop for just £30, my red and black Zenta (which I had to restring to make it left-handed) was a shameless copy of the classic Gibson SG, but without the craftsmanship or quality of the original.

However, this was 1979 and cheap punk rock guitars, made in Japan or Korea and appearing in thousands of newly formed bands up and down the country, seemed to be all the rage.

For when it came to gear, the new punk ideology was almost entirely dismissive of pedigree and reputation. *'Any guitar and any bass drum'* as The Jam sang in *When You're Young*. Weller was right. Who cared what brand of guitar, bass or drum kit you had?

Expensive gear was the preserve of ageing prog rockers who could afford synthesizers and almost certainly read *Melody Maker,* the music weekly dubbed 'Monotony Maker' for its in-depth exclusives on Yes and Genesis. Punk, on the other hand, was DIY music made with the most basic tools on offer. Attitude came before ability.

I didn't have a guitar hero or aspire to become one. I had no interest in mastering *Stairway To Heaven* or the solo in *Bohemian Rhapsody* like so many seemed anxious to do. Instead, hastily formed bands like ours would shun the notion of musical virtuosity or even the existence of popular lyrics or palatable melodies.

Instead, we were more interested in making up droll or shocking band names and indulging in fantasy line ups for them. We designed our own fanzines and home-made badges and, typical of bedroom dreamers like us, wrote an imaginary first album.

My first band, BBC5, were barely even formed before we announced our debut LP *A Different Channel.* The name was my classmate Alex's idea. Remember there were only three television channels in the late-1970s. Five analogue channels (let alone the hundreds of digital ones there are today) would have been as improbable as the idea of going to Paris for the day or being able to read *The Times* on a portable telephone. Five different channels were pretty bloody alternative, which of course we undoubtedly were too.

As it turned out, there were four of us, not five as we might have hoped; me on guitar, my classmate, Alex, on bass and his thirteen-year-old brother, Miguel, who was enlisted on drums.

The bespectacled Eddie, a brilliant footballer who I had befriended in the third form, was on lead vocals – or at least he said he was. We weren't even sure if he could actually sing a note and, logistically, he lived a long way from the rest of us near the Medway towns in Kent.

Nevertheless, he seemed to fancy himself as the next Johnny Rotten and had the required swagger for a frontman. More crucially, he had just bought a Harrington, the casual sports jacket with signature tartan lining once popularised by the fictional character Rodney Harrington in the television series *Peyton Place*.

Of course, we had no business comparing ourselves to The Beatles, but I rather fancied myself as the Paul McCartney figure of the band. This was largely because I was left-handed and wrote stuff down in a song book that I had previously used for my trumpet lessons. Alex, who had an exotic dark complexion on account of his mother being Spanish and whose thick dark hair was worn in sort of a punky pudding bowl, was most definitely George. Mum said he looked like a matador. The cock sure Eddie would, I suppose, have been John.

The fact that none of us could play our instruments properly – not to mention the fact that some of us were shortly to sit our O-Level examinations – didn't appear to deter us one bit in our desire to join our heroes The Stranglers, The Clash, Generation X and others on the London gig circuit.

As the band's guitarist, I put away the old squash racket that I had been using as a guitar and bass substitute and earnestly began learning some chord shapes.

In those days there was no rock and roll YouTuber to talk you through Joy Division's *Transmission* or *Metal Postcard* by Siouxsie and The Banshees. Our school certainly didn't have a tutor for this kind of thing. Back then, Brit schools or rock academies were as fanciful as online computer gaming or a decaf *macchiato* with a shot of vegan friendly salted caramel syrup. Instead, we would leaf cheekily through the song sheets on display in the Chappell Music shop in Bond Street or at a more local music outlet in Lewisham's shopping centre, making drawings in a note pad of some basic chord patterns.

It was hard going at first. The tough and workmanlike metal strings of my Zenta were rusty and unresponsive, and the dodgy action (the gaping chasm between the strings and the fretboard) meant I had to press down extra hard with my non-strumming fingers. I developed rock hard fingertips in the process.

Thanks largely to sheet music for the Buzzcocks, The Sex Pistols and The Jam, I soon had D, A and G major sorted and then wrote my first song *Grin and Bear It* with the very same chords. It went something like this:

I can't always do what I want to do
But I don't mind I've never wanted to
Tear apart and be a star
At that point things just go too far

Another early effort of mine seemed to have it in for viewers of light entertainment. I never did like soap operas:

The TV morons sit by their screens
Coronation Street's on the screen
False characters make them laugh
But we know it's just a farce

This wide-eyed, largely girl-less period (our sex education involved a science teacher doing something with a test tube and a condom) in which the band was almost entirely a fictional entity, produced further songs; the Beatle-ish *Fate,* the Pete Shelley-esque *If It's Anything* and the more rabble-rousing *Tribal Warfare*, which could have passed for a Sham 69 B-side.

I would hear complete songs in my head with the whole band playing their parts vigorously and then sing these two-minute wonders into my portable cassette tape recorder. Next, I would play the crude recordings to my fellow band members through the receiver on my parents' landline.

"Hello?"

"Hi, Alex, it's me. Do you wanna hear the new one? It's called *Only Just Begun*."

"Yeah, sure."

"Okay, here goes then: *one, two three, four…da, da, da-da-da, da, da, da-da-da, da, da, da-da-da, da, da, da-da*."

I wasn't impressing my teachers much at school nor was I imposing all this teenage bluster on my parents. But when it came to my new musical project, I had the drive and the nerve of a Tin Pan Alley huckster. I imagined I could have sweet talked my way into the office of a leading music publisher. I felt I could hum a fresh melody that would one day charm the whole of radioland.

Having access to a landline, even if it was one by your parents' bedside, was an essential tool in a teenager's armoury and, if used correctly, would lead to much creative debate with fellow band members and even dates with girls, assuming the parent who picked up the receiver put you through.

The Post Office, the telecommunications company who owned the line, obviously knew this and came up with the service Dial-a-Disc so that, in a crude forerunner of today's digital steaming services, teenagers would spend hours on the line listening to their favourite tunes.

I would dial 160 in the hope of hearing the latest singles by The Boomtown Rats or The Undertones but, more often than not, would be treated instead to a tinny-sounding loop of *Lay Down Sally* by Eric Clapton or Carol Bayer Sager's *You're Moving Out Today*.

By the 1980s the service was dealing with 200 million calls a year, many of them from public phone boxes. That's a tidy revenue stream indeed for the company that became British Telecom in 1980.

Incidentally, our own home landline number was strangely similar to that of the local Samaritans hotline, which meant that callers would occasionally begin by saying they weren't feeling very well. It seemed cruel to have to brush them off with the standard "Sorry wrong number", so I would listen to the monotone of these depressed voices before eventually admitting my lack of professional insight. Luckily for them, my mum had written the correct number for the Samaritans in pencil on the wall next to our phone. I duly passed it on.

Having a few self-penned songs ready to go was all very well, but when the band finally did get to rehearse the result was a little underwhelming, to say the least.

Obvious musical deficiencies aside, the drums drowned out the feeble guitars and the weedy unamplified vocals, while Alex repeatedly played his overly complicated bass lines at a tempo of his own devising.

We tried a few cover versions from the song sheets that Alex had nicked from the music shop in Lewisham; *Pretty Vacant*, *In The City* and *Babylon's Burning*, but even these fine punk tunes petered out after we all got lost somewhere in the middle.

After only our third get together, an elderly neighbour alerted a noise abatement officer to record the volume levels emanating from my parents' home, where our musical hardware was now installed. This, despite the fact we had put home-made pads on the snare drum, some used eggboxes on the wall and several inches of carpet underlay over the room's skylight.

Bizarrely, there was no banging on the window or irate shouts of "Turn it down!" just a cold and officious letter from the council which landed on our doormat one day.

Even stranger was a message from another neighbour from the flats next door. The bearded middle-aged man, who was usually seen in a black sheepskin coat and matching Astrakhan hat, wanted us to record him a demo tape of our music. He claimed he was in films and was looking for a band to write and record some songs for a new movie he was helping to produce. But having handed over our carefully recorded cassette tape we heard nothing back.

Apparently, once this mysterious character had eventually vacated the flat, the landlord found traces of animal blood on the carpet. It was suggested that he had been involved in witchcraft and sacrificial rituals and had repeatedly woken the elderly couple below with his late-night shenanigans. Justice done, I thought. Serves them right for complaining about our band rehearsal.

Image-wise, we were sending out several mixed messages about our repertoire. Me with drainpipe black trousers (surprisingly hard to get hold of in 1979), a borrowed Burton's jacket from dad's wardrobe and unruly wavy hair which went over the ears.

Alex, meanwhile, would turn up to rehearsals in an olive-green army jumper wearing outdated Kickers boots and an inside out school blazer with some home-made punk badges running down both lapels. At Sam's eighteenth birthday party, where BBC5 were invited to perform in my mum's kitchen, he wore an oversized floor length mac and Chairman Mao style cap. I'm sure my sister's friends would have been happier dancing to the Bob Marley album we had bought specially for the occasion, but instead they had to endure my song *Grin and Bear It* and the two-chord dirge of *Sixteen* by the Buzzcocks.

Drummer Miguel, who was barely into his teens, looked as if his mum had dressed him with his flared jeans and Lacoste tennis shirt. One guitarist, who was with the band only briefly, even had greasy shoulder length hair and professed to liking prog rock. No-one actually *liked* prog rock.

In an ideal world we would have resembled The Rolling Stones in the cool black and white shot I found inside my gatefold double LP *Get Stoned*. Taken, I would have guessed, around 1965, it is almost the perfect band photo with the boys positioned artfully on what looks like the entrance to a magistrate's court.

Another look I was hoping we might channel was Blondie's NYPD-style line up from the back of my *Plastic Letters* LP. Debbie smouldered in black in between Chris and Clem and, strangely, rhythm guitarist Frank 'The Freak' Infante doesn't make it to the photo shoot. But, over to the right, keyboardist James 'Jimmy' Destri seemed to have his image firmly under control with a sort of outgrown French crop and short zip up leather jacket. The casual smouldering cigarette did the rest.

In stark contrast, the BBC5 line up must have looked like Jimmy Pursey junior and his mates or, at best, a more streetwise but admittedly less diverse *Kids From Fame*.

Undeterred by our dubious fashion choices, our brush with the occult and the near catastrophic neighbourhood noise ban, the band continued to commit to the regular Sunday afternoon sessions.

We eventually reached a point where we could proficiently perform twelve of our own songs plus a few easy-to-play cover versions such as *Watcha Gonna Do About it?* by the Small Faces and the three-chord punk/new wave hit *Is Vic There?* by Department S.

I was giving it my very best shot singing lead vocals after Eddie repeatedly failed to show up to rehearsals, but we desperately needed someone else to front up as we headed into a slightly bluesier direction, signalled by our cover of *Come On* by The Rolling Stones, which itself was a cover of a Chuck Berry tune.

Enter my childhood friend, Michael, who now called himself Mick and wore a sharp mod tonic suit which had a harmonica poking out of its left breast pocket. With Mick now singing half the numbers and extending each one timewise with his exuberant blues harp solos, I was able to step back to where I truly belonged. I was thrilled to be the shy and interesting one somewhere to the side of the stage. And, under our new name, Small Print, we showcased our new improved material at the school's Battle of the Bands contest alongside the likes of Dud Czech, The FBI and The Jimmy Nipper Five. There was a decent sized crowd that night and we even got to do an encore. For once I was getting the recognition I felt I deserved.

Indeed, only the week after, one of the school's hard nuts came right up to me during the lunch break. I thought he was going to wallop me.

"You were bloody great," he said, giving me a friendly thump on the arm. "The best thing about the whole night!"

Some other new acolytes from the year below were similarly impressed.

"I really enjoyed your set. Did you see us dancing at the front?" gushed one.

"Yeah, and you lot doing *Is Vic There?* was a stroke of genius," added his mate enthusiastically. "I mean, that record's only been out a couple of weeks!"

In fact, the school concert went sufficiently well for us to approach a youth club just outside Bromley who paired us with Orpington punks Hepatitis Risk, so named because one of their mums, who worked as a nurse, gave them hundreds of free stickers with their oven ready band name on.

And with added soul influenced material like *Go!*, *Run Run Run* and *Taking A Chance*, we were slowly but surely starting to play, and look, like a proper band should.

Out went the scruffy army jumpers and ill-fitting 1970s jackets with home-made pin badges. In came a 2 Tone-inspired wardrobe of dark glasses, plain black shirts and natty hats.

Next up was an invitation by a local fanzine to play at their launch party inside the Chislehurst Caves, the mysterious network of medieval chalk mines which were previously used as both a World War Two air raid shelter and a venue for skiffle and rock bands. Rock monsters Led Zeppelin had, several years earlier, held a party there to launch their record label Swan Song. The debauched Halloween party featured nuns in suspenders serving drinks, a woman in a coffin covered in jelly and some naked male wrestlers.

There was no such entertainment laid on for us, but we got to load our equipment onto a motorised trolley which, with us clinging on for dear life, disappeared into a pitch-black tunnel and eventually emerged at a large candlelit hall complete with its very own stone age stage. Wow, we all thought, grabbing our gear from the trolley in the freezing cold air.

After we played our brief set, a girl in a military style jacket with pretty shoulder length hair came up to me and asked about the band. In all the excitement, I forgot to ask her for her telephone number. This proves the theory that just about anyone can have sex appeal, just as long as they are seen strumming an electric guitar on a public stage.

Critically speaking, our performances were hardly going to trouble members of The Clash or even the Tom Robinson Band, but these early outings were relative triumphs compared to the time we spent waiting in vain to appear during an all-day Rock Against Racism* bill in a Beckenham park. And later at Brixton's Town Hall for a benefit concert organised by the Young Socialists.

*Anti-racism movement formed in response to the rising National Front and comments made by rock star Eric Clapton in support of Enoch Powell's so-called 'Rivers of Blood' speech. A concert headlined by The Clash in Victoria Park, Hackney, attracted a crowd of 80,000 in 1978.

The latter event was headlined by home-grown roots reggae giants Aswad and was attended by hundreds of Jamaican reggae fans, including several local Rastafarians who gathered around the bone-shaking sound system to the rear of the hall. Despite the many promises of Mick's bearded brother-in-law, Al, who as a leading light in the Trotskyist Militant faction had brokered the deal, there just didn't seem to be a slot for us.

As a result, on my seventeenth birthday, I was close to throwing in the towel on this rewarding but increasingly complex musical journey.

"That's it, I'm finished with this!" I announced from the back of Mick's dad's camper van coming back from Brixton.

"What d'yer mean?" Mick snapped back.

"I've had enough. We've spent five bloody hours waiting to get on and then nothing. Fuck them all!"

"Yeah, slightly annoying," Alex interjected, "but there was really nothing we could do about it."

"No one told us it was reggae night!" It was Miguel whose head had appeared from behind a large bass cabinet to the rear of the vehicle. His voice was just starting to break.

"To be honest, lads, I don't think you would have gone down that well," added Al, whose barmy idea this was in the first place.

"I mean, let's be realistic," he continued in his preachy and patronising tone. "If *you* had paid decent money to see the mighty Aswad but instead had to watch a bunch of middle-class tossers like yourselves, you wouldn't like it one bit."

"Yeah," I replied, gritting my teeth, "we would have gone down worse than a visit from the boys in blue."

My churlish words were almost prophetic. Just a few months later, Brixton town centre would explode into violence and public disorder following the police's continued use of 'stop and search' methods against members of the local community. Bloody Saturday on 11th April 1981 left the so-called front line a scene of devastation with dozens of looted shops and rows of smouldering properties. Nearly 300 police officers were injured in the course of making 82 arrests.

"Nothing, but nothing, justifies what happened," replied Prime Minister Margaret Thatcher when asked whether unemployment and racism had played a part in the escalating violence.

On another occasion, we managed to secure a promising booking at a youth club in Feltham, way out in West London not far from Heathrow Airport. "It's a real friendly place," said the promoter over the phone, who was actually going to pay us. "We get a fantastic crowd on Thursdays. Everyone parks their shiny scooters up outside – you'll see!"

Having persuaded my classmate 'Welsh Pete' to drive us all the way there in his parents' van, we all met straight after school, setting off just before the rush hour and arriving at Feltham in perfect time for the sound check. Driver Pete took his stripey tie off but remained in his school uniform throughout.

Indeed, a sizeable crowd had formed by the time the club's DJ announced us onto the stage. The trouble was that a large contingent was wearing eight-hole Dr Martens boots and had severely cropped hair.

There was a lot of pushing and shoving directly in front of us and our second number *Run Run Run*, which we thought sounded a lot like The Jam, was ruined by repeated cries of "Heil Hitler!" Then one of the yobs showered Alex with the contents of his full lager glass and all hell broke loose. "Skinhead, skinhead, skinhead!" they began to chant menacingly, turning their latent aggression on each other as we looked on in bewilderment. Perhaps they mistook us for The Angelic Upstarts or The Cockney Rejects.*

Afterwards, we gathered outside the club house with its council run football pitches and circular clay running track for a necessary debrief.

"Fascists!" said Mick.

"Yeah, what a bunch of c***s," I chipped in, looking carefully over my shoulder.

"Hey, Alex," I added, just to lighten the mood, "that nice new jacket of yours got a right old soaking, didn't it!"

---

*Two bands associated with the then prevalent *Oi!* scene. A reaction largely to the artier pretensions of punk, *Oi!* was championed by journalist Garry Bushell (later a tabloid columnist) in the music weekly *Sounds*.

We all laughed, but this moment was a kind of watershed moment for us all. Not just musically but politically and ideologically too.

Although you wouldn't be able to detect it in our lyrics, at least two of our number were committed socialists and, unlike me, they knew exactly whose side they were on. Alex was a member of the Socialist Workers Party, read the *Morning Star* newspaper and stuck Rock Against Racism posters up at school. Meanwhile Mick had started to hang out with a new crowd from the Labour Party Young Socialists; people who drank real ale and rolled their own cigarettes. People who were one hundred percent committed to kicking out the Tories.

Much as I tried, I could never really understand the small ideological differences between such radical groups with their ever-changing fringe factions and baffling acronyms, SWP, LPYS, RCP, WRP and CPGB. Or as the dub reggae poet Linton Kwesi Johnson put it so succinctly in his 1979 track *Independent Intavenshan*:

The SWE can't set we free
The IMG can't do it for we
The communist party
Cho' them too arty-farty
And the labour rights men
Not go fight for your rights

Whatever left-of-centre umbrella my friends chose to shelter under, they sure didn't like 'Fatcher'.

'The causes (of the recent disturbances in our inner cities),' wrote Mick in my prototype 1980 fanzine *Get Ready!* ('Poems, Riots, 45's review'), *'have been the escalation in the Tories (sic) view of people as a whole because the government seem to take a view that people are a complete non-entity and they hav'nt (sic) got any human existence what so ever 'cos they're casting in the media all about hooligans etc…these people are unemployed, they're (sic) schools are being cut back, they've not been offered University places, youth clubs are being cut down by the cuts that this governments composing, and their (sic) generally being harassed by the government in this way.'*

Miguel and I were less politically inclined having bonded at a large

CND rally in Hyde Park with the frank admission we were "only there for the bands".

Even with the relatively cosseted south London upbringings such as ours, violence was never far from our everyday experience. Going to gigs, especially with a floppy fringe and dressed in a knee-length US army trench coat and pointy suede shoes from Shelly's would mean running the gauntlet of the local yobs' network.

Walking home from school one afternoon a skinhead, still dressed in his school blazer, cracked me flush on the skull with a sharpened rock after failing to get my bus fare from me. Ouch, did that hurt!

Partly hair-raisingly scary and partly electrifying and life affirming, I had witnessed both punch ups and running battles on the football terraces but was never actually the victim, until the day I was randomly set upon by Millwall fans while out browsing the record racks at HMV in Lewisham. Millwall fans had something of a 'reputation', which only seemed to grow after the screening of a 1977 *Panorama* documentary that focused largely on Harry The Dog and his fearsome F-Troop based at their home ground, The Den.

"Give us your scarf," said the youngest. A mere runt in a ten-strong group of scrotes pointing to my Manchester United souvenir given to me for Christmas by my sister.

"No, it's mine."

"Go on, give it to me!"

"No, fuck off."

"Do you want aggro?"

"Er…"

The mob reappeared at WHSmith where I hoped I would be able to finally shake them off.

"Go on, give us your scarf."

"No!"

"Go on, give us the facking scarf!"

Not even the tactic of retreating to the craft and hobbies magazine display could save me as the punches rained down and blood began pouring from my bruised gums staining the sorry red and white polyester that clung defiantly to my neck.

Youth tribes were in abundance on the streets of London and, all too easily, you could run into the wrong crowd at the wrong time. The punks who had been in the ascendancy since 1977 were slightly on the wane by the time I was old enough to go to gigs and would soon mutate into goths or those cheery, cider-swilling punks you would see on the Kings Road up until the 1990s, and possibly even today, with their bright green Mohicans and studded leather biker jackets.

The dreaded skins, all too many of them Nazi sympathisers, didn't look too kindly upon artier new wave types like us. We were chased by a pair of these thugs all the way to the tube at Walthamstow after a New Order gig.

Taking even greater risks in the London night were the soon-to-emerge New Romantics. I had seen their striking outfits on ITV's youth television programme *20th Century Box*, the episode in which Spandau Ballet played an exclusive show at The Scala cinema in King's Cross. Becoming one sounded easy enough, but you needed the balls to steal your mum's blusher and then find something iconic to wear on the train to Charing Cross: a Scotch kilt, a nun's habit or even an iridescent Zoot suit left over from the jazz age.

A social anthropologist might think there was a natural enmity between all the various youth cults and that their followers had strict and highly definable loyalties to the tribe. Far from it. In fact, dipping in and out of these tribes was both common practice and a savvy survival technique, meaning you could identify as a mod one week then reappear several weeks later as a rockabilly or a soul boy. One minute you were into Sham 69 and The Swell Maps, the next it was Secret Affair, The Stray Cats or Simple Minds. You could hardly accuse the music scene of being boring.

In this colourful parade of subcultures, you could also add rastas, hippies (still going strong ten years after Woodstock), heavy metalheads and even the Sloane Rangers of SW3. Personally, I was happy to avoid categorisation of any kind and was guilty of cherry-picking styles from a number of these groups, hence the floppy fringe, the US army trench coat and the silly pointy shoes from Shelly's.

Regional variants were also available. On a day trip to Manchester in 1978 I marvelled at a gang of football fans in the Lowry-esque streets outside Old Trafford. One boy sported dyed orange Ziggy Stardust hair and make-up but with the incongruity of huge bell-bottomed jeans worn with shiny brown bovver boots.

Later that day, while changing trains at Crewe station, I observed a party of immaculate teddy boys and girls who, in their velvet collared drape jackets and heavy brothel creepers, looked like they had stepped out of 1958.

The ones you really had to watch out for, however, were representatives of our very same generation known as 'straights'. A harder group to define sartorially and culturally, but undoubtedly more numerous in the high street or in the workplace, especially north of Watford; this particular tribe sported shoulder length hair, often permed, with a short, workmanlike moustache. Grey Farah slacks and a V-neck waffle-knit jumper completed the ensemble. They probably didn't like music at all.

Influenced by Harp and Skol lager, as well as strong alpha male role models such as Burt Reynolds and Graeme Souness, they would not have hesitated to beat to a pulp hapless young posers like me and my friends should we have found ourselves in the wrong pub at closing time.

As 1980 approached, yet another year closer to the Orwellian 1984, I wrote what I thought was a quite prescient song called *Wake Up, It's The Eighties!* Economic gloom was all around us (unemployment was to hit the three million mark by the end of the year), but the band soldiered on valiantly making a professional demo tape recorded on New Year's Day at a cheap and cheerful basement studio around the back of the Mount Pleasant sorting office in Clerkenwell. Thinking of the bigger picture, Alex brought along two girl backing singers – Bromley girls Steph and her school mate Tracy – to the studio and we even tried two drummers just as Adam and the Ants had already done to great effect.

Lord knows what our parents made of all this creative enterprise, or time wasting as they should have called it out. To any sensible observer, it would seem that I was deliberately sabotaging my hopes of getting good enough grades to enter a leading university, which tragically turned out to be the case.

Being in the band was just about the only thing that sustained me. It was an empowering choice of hobby that helped me to grow in confidence. It made me a more outgoing personality too, but at what cost?

And tolerant and loving as they were, I'm sure my mum and dad were not remotely impressed by my increasingly disturbing school reports. Or by having to turn up to Bromley Police Station one Saturday afternoon after three of us had been detained for alleged shoplifting at the Wing Music shop on the London Road.

"We're not the mafia, you know," I spat back at the station sergeant standing in front of me.

The police officer's job was to unravel the mystery behind why one of Wing Music's Marshall bass cabinets had gone walkabouts as I bothered one of the assistants with inane questions about second-hand microphones.

Of course, the three founding members of Small Print had no connection whatsoever to the Sicilian-based crime syndicate, yet understandably might have given a faint impression there indeed was an already carefully constructed plot to boost the wattage of the band's sorry looking backline.

"Well, sonny," the station sergeant countered, "we've just rang your parents and right now they're on their way to pick you up."

I gulped. The officer looked deadly serious. It probably wasn't how mum and dad imagined their Saturday afternoon would go.

"You know, if I was your old man," he added, "you'd already be through that brick wall behind you instead of trying to be such a *fucking smart arse*!"

Thankfully, none of us were formally charged with the alleged theft and we were able to move on quickly from this shameful episode. But, in broader terms, the incident fully encapsulated the downside of growing up in a time that people still regard as a 'golden era' of alternative music and pop culture. Perhaps, it explains, why there is a best-selling t-shirt bearing the slogan 'Punk Rock Ruined My Life'.

Never mind the needless deaths of Sid and Nancy or the awful suicide of Joy Division's Ian Curtis, just how many other promising careers were derailed by the turbulent jet stream of punk and new wave?

On reflection, it was worth it for seeing Joy Division play *Love Will Tear Us Apart* at a small club in West Hampstead shortly before Ian Curtis departed. It was also exciting to tap into the energy of so many new wave and post-punk bands at the legendary Marquee Club, or even sing and play the electric guitar myself in a real recording studio.

No, punk rock did not ruin my life, but if this most vital and hard-to-ignore music movement hadn't come along, I believe I would have passed more easily through those most challenging teenage years. Maybe I would have dedicated my time and energy more enthusiastically to deep and serious learning. Maybe I would have embraced other more collegiate activities such as drama, sport or even singing in the school choir. Maybe my progression into the adult world would have been a smoother one.

Unavoidably, a new decade was just around the corner. All would be revealed.

9.

ABSOLUTE BEGINNERS

"Dan, it's for you."

Mum was calling me from downstairs. Somebody wanted to speak to me on the phone.

"Hello, who is it?" I asked, putting the receiver to my ear.

"It's me, Miguel," said the voice at the other end. "I need to come over and talk to you about something. Do you think I could call round later?"

"Yeah, sure," I said. "I'm supposed to be going out tonight but around six or seven o'clock is fine."

Miguel, I thought, I wonder what he wants. When the band had broken up the summer before, we had all gone our separate ways. Alex had done rather better in his A-Level exams than I had and was at university in Norwich reading English Literature. He had already had a few articles published in both political and fringe arts magazines and seemed to be on course for a life in journalism or politics, or maybe both.

Miguel, two years younger, was attending sixth form college and was playing in a punk/funk band called Zero Beat. At the same time, Mick was living in a flat in East Greenwich with an older girlfriend he had met with his group of Young Socialists. Mick and I weren't the best of friends anymore, but occasionally he would invite me to one of his pub gigs where, squeezed into the same tonic jacket, he would deliver those same spirited harmonica bursts.

Soon enough there was a knock on the door.

"Mig, how the hell are you?"

He smiled at me weakly.

"I'm not coming in," he said, "I simply had to tell you."

"Tell me what?"

He sighed, then stared briefly at the front step before continuing.

"I'm sorry, but there's no other way of saying this. Alex is dead."

Still standing in the doorway, I checked Miguel's expression for signs this might be some terrible mistake. Perhaps this was some sort of bizarre practical joke. We used to enjoy pulling pranks on people, such as the time the three of us lay in the road pretending to be dead, only to run off giggling when the concerned motorist stopped to investigate.

I might have expected him to announce, "So do you wanna join Zero Beat?", "My girlfriend's pregnant" or "We're all moving to Spain" but not "ALEX IS DEAD".

"Er, so do you wanna come in?" I felt sorry for him standing there waiting for me to react.

"No, that's okay," he said, regaining his composure. "There are a few more of Alex's friends who don't know the news yet. I really should go off and tell them."

Alex, it transpired, was staying overnight at an acquaintance's flat where there was a lethal carbon monoxide leak. He never woke up.

His funeral, only a few weeks later, was a surreal occasion. Dark clouds hung over the cemetery outside Norwich and the incessant rain lashed the squat stones that sprung out of the ground. Legions of shellshocked young punks – the alternative gang Alex had always craved – filed into the chapel to pay their respects. Miguel bravely stood up at the front and read his eulogy. We then watched Alex's coffin disappear into the cremation chamber to the sound of Joy Division's *Atmosphere*.

Not that long ago, Alex and I had been willing converts to the cult indie band standing side-by-side in the Rainbow's vast auditorium to hear the same dark but uplifting music. Now he was lying motionless in that dreadful wooden box and on his way to oblivion. Poor Alex. He didn't really stand a chance as he lay crashed out on his friend's sofa.

Early one morning in July 1980, a group of kids from the Blitz Club in London, including the club's front man and New Romantic style leader, Steve Strange, gathered on a stony beach near Hastings in East Sussex. They had been specially invited by their hero, David Bowie, who was here to shoot his latest pop video *Ashes To Ashes*, a record-breaking £250,000 production by the director, David Mallet.

Each was paid £50 in cash for the trouble which must have seemed a reasonable enough amount to these Bowie acolytes. After all, this was a just another excuse for indulging in some fancy dress and, as Bowie had joked with them before the shoot began, they would be heroes just for one day.

The video, which included dystopian colour tinted scenes of the singer dressed as an Italian Pierrot followed closely by some mysterious figures in black and, behind them, a menacing looking bulldozer, was loaded with symbolism, religious or otherwise.

The disconcerting beach scene was intercut with clips of Bowie in a padded cell and later in a wrecked space capsule which looked like something from the film *Alien* by Ridley Scott.

All seemed to be going smoothly until the shoot was, annoyingly, held up by an elderly local man who was out walking his dog. As Bowie and his bizarrely clad Blitz coterie continued their solemn march towards the camera, the dog walker had the temerity to put himself and his canine companion directly into the frame.

"Excuse me!" the exasperated video director shouted out to the man. "Do you know who this is?"

The man turned around to have a better look at the Thin White Duke. Bowie was in the throes of yet another reinvention having released the LP *Heroes* and *Lodger*, the 1979 album that incorporated Hijaz Non-Western musical scales and the use of Brian Eno's *Oblique Strategies* cards.

"Yeah, of course I do," surmised the man.

"Well, who is it then?"

"It's some c**t in a clown suit."

My own reality check occurred when my mum suggested that I looked up my old careers officer, the bald, tigger-ish one who had visited our school and asked us a series of multiple-choice questions, which resulted in a multi-paged computer printout telling me I would mostly be suited to a career as a social worker. As if!

His office was an echoey room housed in an old LCC (London County Council) school at the very top end of the Old Kent Road. On his desk there was simply a telephone and a Rolodex with some steel filing cabinets lined up behind him.

"I understand that you're looking for a job," he said gesturing to the empty chair in front of his desk.

"Yes, I am."

He reached into one of the draws behind him and pulled out a selection of printed cards. "Hmm," he said, "I might just have something for you. There's a firm of solicitors in Holborn here, they're looking for an office junior. Shall I give them a call for you?"

I nodded as enthusiastically as I could. Was this the alternative rock and roll life I had been dreaming of only a few months earlier? Was this the end of the teenage dream I had so masterfully conjured up out of nothing?

I sat as the careers officer had a word with someone at the chambers. As he spoke on the phone, he looked at me while replying mostly in the affirmative to the voice on the other line.

"Yes, he can start now…no, he doesn't need to give an employer notice…yes, he has a national insurance number."

And, after the briefest of brief interviews a couple of days later, I was hired. Congratulations were in order. I had segued seamlessly from 'shy and interesting' guitar player and reluctant sixth former to salaried office dogsbody.

As an office temp during the school summer holidays, I had already had a taste of the white-collar workplace. Going to one involved sharing a packed and lumbering suburban train with frustrated commuters a bit like my dad. Stale cigarette smoke clung to dandruff-flecked Polyester suits and liveried grey British Rail seats, following you all the way to the office where clunky GPO telephones and crystal glass ashtrays took pride of place on austere mahogany desks. Tea came from an urn wheeled around the office by a char lady while coffee, if you could actually brave one, came from a Styrofoam cup in the staff kitchen.

For a smooth tasting hit of caffeine, you simply poured the contents of a plastic kettle onto a bitter-tasting heap of Maxwell House. *Et voila!* Lunch, meanwhile, was invariably a toasted cheese sandwich, made with obligatory sliced white bread and paid for with Luncheon Vouchers.

Offices seemed to me just like schools with their strict hierarchies, in this case an eco-system divided into solicitors, trainee solicitors, clerks, secretaries, finance officers and presiding at the top of the chain the three partners of the firm: Nasty, Imperious and Downright Rude.

The days passed predictably enough. I picked up people's post, photocopied pages of legal documents, joined the long queues at the Post Office and flirted with the secretaries. Otherwise, the work was mind-numbingly boring.

The most exciting thing to happen was when they decommissioned my desk so they could install a new fax machine on it. This contraption, which must have been one of the earliest models on the market, was as large and as heavy as an old trunk.

The entire firm gathered around it while, after several high-pitched beeps and intermittent blasts of weird static noise, a one-page letter magically transported itself to an office in Zurich.

In truth, this juncture of my life was very much a barren period; the lowly rung of a slippery career ladder and the deserved result of not working hard enough to impress the exam boards. It was a job, pure and simple, paying me an adequate weekly wage to bide my time and leave home for a shared flat that had woodchip walls and horrible 1970s flowery curtains in pre-gentrified Clapham North.

"What's so great about living in Clapham?" I had asked the rather terse lettings agent in her tiny office above Oxford Circus tube station.

"Clapham?" came the incredulous reply, "Clapham is actually very popular with our clients. It's extremely sought after by City types," she beamed at my flat mate, Billy, who had just started as a trainee in a merchant bank.

"What's more, the flat is only two minutes' walk from the tube station. Any Northern Line train will speed you to the City or the West End in less than half an hour." So that was it, I was officially connected to London's nine to five grid.

Our sleeping capital city, yet to shake off the neglect of the previous decades during which most public buildings were covered in black soot left over from 1950s pea soupers,* wasn't all doom and gloom. And even from the standpoint of my disappointing nine to five I could already spy some promising pockets of resistance.

A friend from school had already introduced me to a noisy back-room night club frequented by art students and cross-dressing outsiders which was accessed through the back of the gay nightclub Heaven under the railway arches at Charing Cross.

This after-hours scene with its aggressive posing and harsh Teutonic dance grooves wasn't entirely for me, and I had to wait on a freezing railway platform for the first commuter train home afterwards.

But with some money now going directly into my pocket I was soon lured to the more red-blooded playgrounds of the Mudd Club, Camden Palace, The Wag, Le Beat Route and the itinerant Dirtbox. These establishments fronted by flamboyant and slightly intimidating style leaders such as Steve Strange, Philip Sallon and Chris Sullivan, reinvigorated many a tired West End dive and brought the crowds back to dilapidated Gin Palaces, old snooker halls and even abandoned industrial warehouses.

The children who had survived that dark and uncertain winter of 1974, and the later punk onslaught, were coming of age and were hell bent on having a party. So what, you may well ask, was the celebration exactly? Who cared. 'Fuck Art, Let's Danse' as the t-shirt slogan said.

The appeal of these night clubs rested largely on them being informal mating arenas, a nocturnal home to elitist tribes with their

*Colloquial term to describe the thick 'London fog' caused by excessive use of domestic and industrial coal. The Great Smog of 1952 resulted in the deaths of around 12,000 Londoners, a disaster which led to the Clean Air Act of 1956.

unique social order comprised of DJ's, pop stars, fashion designers and media types.

At the top of the chain were the club runners themselves who shared both entrepreneurial flair and a genuine love of clothes and music. They had every reason not to let you and your posse inside – too plain, too strait, too old, too blokey, too provincial looking to name just a few excuses – but once you were allowed in, you could be one of the gang.*

Of course, as we pranced around to the after-hours soundtrack of old funk and disco tunes with cheap hairspray holding up our severe looking flat top hairstyles, it dawned upon us that there was no need to grow up after all.

Going to see bands gave way to dancing in nightclubs or, in my case, getting up enough courage to dance. If I did go out for live music, it was now to see predominantly black American artists such as Defunkt, Gil Scot Heron, Was (Not Was) and Grandmaster Flash and the Furious Five, the Bronx outfit responsible for propelling rap music straight to the top of the charts. It was now possible for a young white Londoner to enjoy shared cultural practices (without the racism and the social exclusion obviously) with folks from downtown New York, Chicago or Washington DC.

In boring Clapham, where the pubs were almost exclusively for seasoned Irish drinkers and a few aggressive looking straights who were best avoided, I befriended some fellow West End clubbers; two outrageous party girls called Naomi and Lizzie.

Naomi was as tall and as stop-the-traffic stunning as the *Nightclubbing* singer Grace Jones. Lizzie came from Wales and had a spiky bleached flat top hairdo and drank copious amounts of snakebite and black, the drink made from mixing lager with cider then adding a dash of blackcurrant squash to taste.

They lived in a sprawling squat just behind the high street and we would meet up late at night to catch the outrageous drag act in the Two Brewers pub on the high street, mingling with the clean-cut

*Blitz Club host Steve Strange allegedly turned away Mick Jagger who looked "too normal" in his blue jeans and trainers.

clones in their uniform of checked cowboy shirts, heavy work boots and bristling moustaches.

At weekends we would catch the last tube up to Leicester Square then score some cheap speed off a guy with a huge rockabilly quiff in the Spice of Life pub before heading to various subterranean dives in the West End.

One weekend my new friends helped reinforce my usual amphetamine intake with some pills known as 'blues', or 'French blues' as they were known on the super-charged 1960s club scene. Sailing in and out of nightclubs and word of mouth warehouse parties meant I went without sleep for at least three consecutive nights. It was an experience which left me questioning my own sanity and, towards the end of the high, being unusually chatty and opinionated – possibly even offensive – at work on the Monday.

During the decidedly more mundane working week, the girls who were signing on and receiving dole money would surprise me by turning up at the flat with tales of their adventures. They would speak so fast, a result no doubt of their impressive daily speed intake, that it was practically impossible to follow their drift.

"Well, Dan, there was this rasta guy in the chippie and he drops one of his chips right and then the bloke behind the counter says 'hey you dropped one of your chips' and you're never gonna believe it, Dan, but he actually goes and picks it up off the floor and bloody well eats it…"

I was flattered by the attention, particularly by that of the doting Naomi, who I suppose had become a girlfriend, but found their company way too lively, especially after a long hard day of office drudgery.

When I broke up with Naomi, the pair responded by kicking my moped over. One evening I heard a loud noise outside, so I peaked through the filthy net curtains only to witness the pair scarpering towards the high street, laughing like hyenas as they went.

A doomed romance with an older secretary from work called Karen floundered after I accidentally set fire to the kitchen as I attempted to fry potatoes. Allowing the thick smoke to disappear out of the windows, we both walked to the corner shop to drown our sorrows with some take away chips and some warm Stella Artois from the shop's proprietor who wore an unconvincing wig held together with sticking plaster. You see, when it came to girls, I desperately needed someone to teach me a few valuable lessons. Least of all in the art of introducing myself. My radar for this sort of social interaction was appalling, as demonstrated on an occasion (there were many others) when a foxy Paula Yates lookalike made a beeline for me at a party.

"Hey, haven't I seen you somewhere before?"

I looked her up and down.

"Er…no. I don't think so."

So while still hopeless with girls and looking like an emaciated extra from *On The Waterfront*, my sonic palette gained some colourful new additions. This was hardly surprising as the music around me was decidedly blacker, funkier and increasingly more synthesised.

American rap and funk records soon began to take pride of place in my record collection, augmented by some old disco and soul 45 rpms that I had found going for a just few pennies in Hanway Street or at Beano's, the second-hand vinyl store in downtown Croydon.

I joined some friends from South London for a return ferry and train trip to Amsterdam where we smoked huge reefers and blasted out the latest New York hip hop tunes from an absurdly large boom box. Unsurprisingly, this didn't entirely meet with the approval of the locals.

As we got lost in the maze of streets in and around the Jordaan, an inquisitive middle-aged man dressed in a cheesecloth shirt approached us.

"Hey, you guys! Could you turn that music down a bit?"

"What?"

I'm the lady romancer, I'm the cool fly guy, I'm the lady chaser, I'm the rhyme creator…

"Open your eyes and ears to all the things around you instead. Do you understand what I'm talking about?"

When I say a def rhyme, you never hear one greater, like a hip hop, a little hi-wop a dop, listen to me T-Ski, while I rock the spot…

"Sorry?"

"What I mean to point out is that you should leave behind the things you already have at home. Don't you think that travel is an opportunity to embrace your new environment?"

"Eh?"

"I mean, just look around, you guys! You could be sensible by turning that loud noise off. Listen to the sound of Amsterdam instead!"

"Can't hear you."

It's the B-B-E-E-A-A-T-T-T-T-T-T-T in your mind and your body – catch the beat!

If I could sum up this era in the grooves of one 12-inch vinyl record it would surely be *Let The Music Play* by the Brooklyn based singer Shannon. Best heard on a top of the range sound system, or better still in a club, this relentless dance anthem with its irresistible opening *'we started dancing and love put us into a groove'* seemed to combine the very best of American soul music with the latest hard driven beats and basslines (courtesy of Roland's TB-303 bass synthesizer) also heard on records by pioneering hip hop artists Whodini or Afrika Bambaataa.

Coming a close second to this would be *Walking On Sunshine* by the short-lived studio project Rocker's Revenge. With its throbbing dub bass punches, futuristic synth motifs and intoxicating sprinkling of handclaps and congas, this Arthur Baker produced Eddie Grant cover version was ideally suited to our sunshine-filled park outings with the ghetto blaster. Just about every club DJ in town seemed to have a copy of this record.

Such rare, imported sounds, which on Saturday afternoons Billy and I would source from Groove Records, Soho, or City Sounds near the office in Holborn, often clocked in a playing time of seven minutes or more.

Compared with the 'bless my cotton socks I'm in the news' post-punk pop of 1980, these were veritable sonic masterpieces. Admittedly, the underlying messages behind, say, Indeep's *Last Night A DJ Saved My Life* or *I.O.U* by Freeez were hardly profound, but as mini symphonies for our dangerously undernourished souls, they were perfect.

This exciting new dance music, alongside a creeping bebop and Latin jazz revival, gave us a ready-made soundtrack as we rediscovered our crumbling old town carrying copies of *On The Road* or Colin MacInnes's *Absolute Beginners* dressed in the sub-beatnik uniform of a checked shirt and rolled up Levis worn with moccasins or espadrilles *sans* socks.

First published in 1959 as part of his 'London trilogy', and set largely in the west London enclave of Notting Hill, MacInnes's book is a strange work of fiction indeed. A classic outsider's novel which, through the voice of its young narrator, Blitz Baby, plus a colourful cast of friends, including Mr Cool and The Wizard, explores sex, jazz, race and violence in a city just about over the worst of rationing.

This London, with its underground drugs scene, marginalised Caribbean communities and simmering racial tensions, is far from a perfect utopia but reading it as a teenager in the early 1980s, it came across as a bold and convincing manifesto for our city, one which was still very much in a state of transition. Well, isn't it always?

As our narrator reminds his mixed-race friend, Mr Cool, himself a target of the Notting Hill Teddy Boys: "Cool, this is London, not some hick city in the provinces! This is London, man, a capital, a great big city where every kind of race has lived ever since the Romans!"

A passable film musical version of *Absolute Beginners,* directed by Julien Temple who made *The Great Rock 'n' Roll Swindle,* followed in 1986. But unlike the book's protagonist, I had no plans whatsoever to strike a resounding blow for youth against the cynical adult hierarchy. Instead, a kind of quiet contentment came with my ordered working week which was given an important counterpoint by my arguably shallow and destructive weekend clothes and clubbing lifestyle.

And it was around this time that I began to meet girls who, despite my unpromising credentials, seemed interested enough in going out with me.

Apart from Naomi, there was a dalliance with a Danish girl who smoked Winstons, read Arthur C. Clarke and wore a long leather coat, like the French pop singer Francoise Hardy. The trouble was, we kept misunderstanding each other. When she said: "Come and meet me at the entrance of my old school. I'll see you at ten," I arrived hopefully at 10pm in the evening. The place was eerily dark and deserted. My long journey across town had been wasted. She, of course, had been there at ten in the morning. It was hopeless.

Then I met Maxine who latched onto me as I DJ'd at a friend's New Year's Eve party. Maxine had all the hallmarks of a classic 1980s wild child. Exaggerated shows of affection and extravagant generosity were contrasted by her jealous and often irrational rages, and she seemed to have a 'new best friend' and a fresh change of image practically every month.

We didn't see much of each other during the week as she lived for some of the time with her father in Hertfordshire but, every Friday evening, she would appear at my front door in the latest creations from Miss Selfridge and Top Shop. It would be woollen leg warmers and dayglo lipstick one week and the next would be dressed down dungarees and a chic bandana in her hair like the girls from Bananarama. Being in a band and writing songs about my boring life could not have been further from my thoughts.

At my twenty first birthday party, I danced with Maxine and some of my closest friends to the brilliant new Wham! single *Wake Me Up Before You Go Go*. Our breakup tune almost exactly a year later was the lyrically and musically contrasting *When Love Breaks Down* by Prefab Sprout.

Track number four on their second album *Steve McQueen* (the one featuring the band gathered around an old Triumph motorbike) was the only love song that I had really taken to heart.

Power ballads, especially the more radio-friendly ones like Jennifer Rush's *The Power Of Love* or *I Want To Know What Love Is* by Foreigner, were notorious for their clichéd rock arrangements and ridiculous vocal histrionics. In contrast, *When Love Breaks Down* seemed to slowly creep up on you. In place of the clichés and the virtuosity was a measured and almost minimalist approach that expressed complex and sometimes abstract ideas about romance and relationships.

Opening with a simple piano and string motif, the slightly strained singing of Paddy McAloon, aided by the angelic sounding Wendy Smith, enquires early in the song *'have you seen the weather?'* It's as if he were a character from a black and white kitchen sink drama starring Tom Courtenay or Rita Tushingham.

Likewise, he and his easy-going lover, he sings quaintly, are both *'boxing clever'* and *'free as old confetti'*. Like protagonists in an old Hollywood musical they are to *'paint the town'* before, with no shortage of dramatic pathos, their love breaks down.

Just as in the song *Goodbye Lucille #1* (*'ooh Jonny, Jonny, Jonny'*) which has the winning line *'life's not complete 'til your heart's missed a beat'*, songwriter McAloon is singing about his own heartbreak, of course, but his is a thoughtful, tender and universal response to emotional trauma, and one which I still find hugely relatable to today:

'The things you do to stop the truth from hurting you...'

And when Maxine disappeared – people really did disappear in the 1980s – to join some new music biz friends in a shared house somewhere off the Portobello Road (or at least that's what she told me), I was utterly floored by my first taste of heart break. All I could do was mope around my bedroom smoking endless Marlboro Lights with a sick feeling in my stomach and play records such as these. Thanks to the quirky pop funk of Orange Juice or Prefab Sprout with their aching soft rock guitars, inventive rhythm shifts and strange twists of melody, I was provided with a necessary healing balm. Slowly, but surely, I returned to the fray stronger and even more resilient, especially in affairs of the heart.

10.

THIS CHARMING MAN

The old guitar had been leaning idly against my bedroom wall for some time, and I didn't even own an amplifier any more. Would I ever find a new band? And, if so, what kind of music would they be into?

I had jammed a few times with some friends at Sleazy's rehearsal studio. Alighting at Wapping underground station carrying my cheap Les Paul copy, I walked along the cobble stones past the empty spice warehouses inhaling the aroma of pepper and cumin along the way.

Sleazy's was damp and dirty and was run by a bloke called John who we joked was the bar man from the television series *Minder*. We played some Motown covers and something that sounded a bit like Haircut 100 but nothing promising enough came of the sessions to go back and do it properly.

I dug my old trumpet out to play a few gigs with Zero Beat who wanted some snappy brass lines like the ones on the latest Spandau Ballet single. Then, while I waited for a band to come on at The Marquee in Soho, I bumped into someone who was bold enough to call themselves a singer.

"You'll never guess what," announced this stranger, leaning over at the bar crush, "but I've just been recording a track. I did it in a studio with Tom Robinson."

"Oh yeah?"

"Yeah, it's a song I wrote with him called *Essex Girls and Essex Boys*."

"What's *that* about?" I asked, thinking this was an unusual subject for a song.

"Oh, you know," he explained, "I work in the City you see, and I just couldn't help noticing all those commuters from places like Ilford and Romford. They've got their own way of talking and dressing, you know. The girls are all called Debbie or Tina and their geezers like soul music and drive around in souped up Ford Cortinas. It's hilarious!"

"I bet," I said, edging carefully away from the bar with my pint of watery lager.

Tom Robinson. Now that was a credible name to drop. Although his band, the politically driven Tom Robinson Band, were no longer active, Tom Robinson was having some success as a solo artist and his song *War Baby* would reach the dizzy heights of the Top Ten.

"Let me introduce myself, I'm Gavin," he said in between sips of Coca-Cola in a plastic glass. Gavin then reached into an Our Price Records bag and produced a cassette tape.

The cover had a crude photocopied picture of a Mark 1 Ford Cortina glued to the card inlay. The song's title was written directly below it.

With his thick black hair, smart white Fred Perry shirt and regular lapses into East End-ese, Gavin reminded me of the actor Jack Wild from the musical film *Oliver*. This wasn't going to be some dodgy scam, I wondered.

"Have it if you like. See whatcha think. My number's on the back if yer need it."

"Thanks a lot, mate, I'll give it a listen," I said, sliding the tape into the pocket of my olive-green army surplus trench coat.

Walking back down Wardour Street and through Chinatown on my own, I returned home to give it my proper attention. I pressed the play button on my stereo system and out it jumped.

First the jaunty synthetic drum beat and then a *faux* brass motif that immediately put me in mind of Basildon synth pop merchants Depeche Mode:

They come from Harlow, Romford and Grays
They are so different in so many ways
They are a breed all of their own
That's Debbie and Tina, Stevie and Tone

This was fun! Borrowing estuarial vocal stylings from both Ian Dury and Madness, Gavin's vocal was actually rather accomplished, proving he wasn't such a bullshitter after all. And although the music wasn't really my kind of thing, the tune was both melodic and memorable and had something to say in an original and entertaining way. A few days later, I made a point of calling the number written on the back of the cassette cover.

Over the phone we agreed that I should visit his one bedroomed flat in St Katherine's Dock to hear more of his songs. And maybe he would listen to some of my ideas, however loosely formed they were.

This meeting led to the start of a new songwriting collaboration, from which two songs *Come Back With Me* and *You Lead Me On* were demoed in a north London studio. A fully-fledged band was hardly the intention but, somehow, my strumming along to Gavin's handwritten lyric sheets produced more tunes: *Everything and More, Don't Let Me Go Tonight* and *Wonderland* with its mysterious '*Creep in early, feeling dirty, whistle me to sleep...*'

Me, the 'shy and interesting one' had finally found a new foil and I was more than happy to play second fiddle in the partnership. When it came to writing lyrics, I didn't have a clear idea of what I wanted to say but I did enjoy throwing zeitgeisty, politicised phrases into the hat. One bridge I wrote (that all-important link between the verse and the chorus) went: '*The power of the dollar, the might of the pound*'. It sounded amazing with sustained F and G chords underneath it. Another line I was pleased with dealt with the increasing automation of the workplace: '*We are just willing slaves to Japanese technology*'. That fax machine at the solicitor's office must have really made an impression.

Gavin, however, preferred romantic themes, familiar, everyday words and line endings that rhymed (moon/June, stay/away, right/ tonight etc.) so very often my suggestions never made it to the final cut. My *'slaves to Japanese technology'* ended up as *'No more evidence for you to state with confidence'* when we eventually got around to recording the song *Release Me*.

But despite our different approaches to music making, I used to love those trips to his bright modern flat located at the edge of the City on the north side of Tower Bridge. Scaling the flat's long concrete stairwell, guitar case in hand, I would detect the bright chiming guitars of Haircut 100 or Friends Again calling from his kitchen window.

And, as I entered the tight hallway, Gavin would continue to sing along unashamedly before tea and biscuits were served and felt tip pens and sheets of paper were produced from a drawer in his bedroom.

As in any speculative endeavour, optimism is an underrated drug and Gavin had it in spades. Indeed, it wasn't long until our embryonic band found itself with a proper line up and a vague notion, having been spurred on by hearing the brilliant *This Charming Man* by The Smiths, to play guitar-driven indie pop.

Me on guitar, Gavin on lead vocals, untried Clapham neighbour Rob on bass and my old *compañero* Miguel helping out on drums.

Of course, every band needs their own space. Before they were famous The Rolling Stones famously auditioned for new members in a room above a pub in Soho. Radiohead used a converted apple shed in rural Oxfordshire. Led Zeppelin first got together in a Chinatown basement, while The Ramones honed their influential sound from the confines of, you guessed it, a New York garage.

Booking and spending time in paid rehearsal space is, unfortunately, one of the downsides of making music with other people. You can find a studio in a great location and at the perfect time slot for you and your band mates, yet nothing will ever be quite right.

In a large building with several adjoining rehearsal rooms, it is a given that you will hear the band next door's attempts to out rock Metallica or Slipknot with their grungy Marshall stacks turned up to eleven. Either that or there will be an underground train shaking the building's foundations every ten minutes.

Then there are the things that are only marginally more controllable; in-house guitar amplifiers that inexplicably buzz and feedback, microphones that hiss and crackle or, even worse, electrocute you.

Overhead, fluorescent ceiling lights can flicker on and off until you and your band mates go stark raving bonkers.

The airless room you have been appointed will almost certainly smell of the previous band's farts and I guarantee there will be a half-eaten kebab behind the drum kit. One dodgy space I rehearsed in backed onto the kitchen of a neighbourhood restaurant. Perfect, you might suppose, for nipping out for a sandwich mid-rehearsal. The trouble was one of the diner's resident rats scratched its way through the party wall and ran amok behind a bass cabinet until a quick-witted band member, who hung out there to smoke weed, managed to stun the rodent with the heavier end of his electric guitar.

Pete Townsend would have been mightily impressed.

Our first rehearsal space turned out to be an intimate brick lined coal storage area below a town house just off the famous Kings Road in Chelsea. Rob's dad, who lived there, offered it to us under the proviso that we cleared a huge pile of coal along with the mounds of black dust that had, over the years, spread to just about every corner of the cellar.

This task took the most part of a weekend and it wasn't the best remedy for my on/off asthmatic condition, but at least we had a band headquarters of our own with room enough to store some backline amps and a drum kit.

On the subject of drums, what do you call a drummer with half a brain? Gifted.

What does a drummer use for contraception? His personality.

Did you hear about the drummer that finished high school? Me neither.

The men or women stuck behind the kit have often been a source of ridicule among the rock and roll community, often unfairly in my opinion. Miguel bowed out shortly after our first gig at the Central London Polytechnic (where I was now enrolled in a Business Studies course – yes, I know!) to join indie darlings The Beloved on a tour of northern Europe.

His boots were filled by Rory, an amiable but somewhat apprehensive drummer from the wilds of Essex. His music taste, however, was impeccable (The Doors, Love, Scott Walker, Bert Bacharach, The Velvet Underground etc.), and despite the fact that he seemed to be living inside a groovy movie of his own imagination, his softer, more soulful playing had real moments of brilliance.

But on the downside were his sudden and unexplained lapses of concentration. Rory, you see, would literally stop playing mid-song. Looking up from my guitar to see what the fuck was going on, I would observe him staring blankly into space, as if he had seen a ghost.

Rory's clingy, sour-faced girlfriend, Mandy, who joined him on his regular car journeys to the Kings Road, often during the evening rush hour, didn't help. She would sit at the edge of our cramped music dungeon doing word puzzles and scowl in his direction.

Unsurprisingly, he was often late or never turned up at all.

Sadly we had no option but to post an ad for a replacement drummer in the Musicians Wanted section of the *Melody Maker*. That individual, so the wording went, had to play with 'style, charm and commotion'. This offered a clue, insisted Gavin, to our then predominant musical influences: The Style Council, The Smiths and Lloyd Cole and The Commotions.

So in amongst the hopefuls the following week was someone from The June Brides, a milkman from Croydon who played in a pub band, and a University of Hull graduate who claimed to have been friends with fellow students Ben and Tracey from the uber cool jazz/pop duo Everything But The Girl.

"So, who have you been playing with lately?" Gavin asked this last drummer, once he had put his sticks down and accepted the warm bottle of Pils we were offering each applicant. "Oh, you know, just a bit of jamming with friends from uni and, yeah, I helped my dad out a bit with a couple of studio tracks he was recording over the summer."

"Your dad?" asked Rob, "that sounds interesting."

"Yeah," said the drummer, "Dad used to play in The Shadows. Now he's working with some old Sixties dudes on a new cover's album. Sting and Phil Collins popped into the studio to record some vocals. I just did some percussion fills for them in the end."

"Wicked!" I said, with just a hint of sarcasm.

Obviously, we should have offered him the job there and then but, for some reason, we held back. Maybe we didn't like his playing style, his shoes or his shoulder length hair. Could he even have been a bit of a hippie? It's possible we considered it so excruciatingly uncool that he had hung out with rock royalty and mullet haired has-beens like Mike Oldfield and Dire Straits. Collectively, we illustrated perfectly the old George Bernard Shaw saying that 'youth is wasted on the young'.

So, while we skilfully side-stepped the problem of having our drummer being the offspring of someone who had fronted one of the most popular acts of the 1960s, we asked our modest but solid-sounding milkman, who had his own car and a proper looking kit, to return for a callback the following week.

And then we were four.

11.

HEY DJ

We were going to make some fantastic music together and we'd get to play a few live gigs. Maybe we'd find ourselves on the radar of some big record company and then, who knows?

But, first, we needed to find that all-important band name.

Needless to say, names are almost entirely subjective affairs with members rarely agreeing unanimously on those word or number configurations that, with a bit of luck, will end up embossed at the centre of a real recorded disc.

Occasionally, both the music and the brand collide perfectly: The Smiths, De La Soul, Camper Van Beethoven. At other times the band members overthink it all and score an embarrassing own goal: Def Leppard, Butthole Surfers, Limp Bizkit.

Remember also that some of the most successful bands of all time have really quite terrible names: Nirvana, Oasis, Arctic Monkeys, The Weeknd and many others besides.

By coming up with the name Illicit Kiss for our own musical venture, I'm prepared to admit we got this one wrong. Gavin, who was gay but not completely out of the closet, came up with the idea. Perhaps Illicit Kiss chimed with his song lyrics that often alluded to secret loves and unrequited passions across crowded rooms. Like Morrissey, he rather fancied himself as a latter-day Oscar Wilde. Maybe it was an attempt also to evoke the ever-so-seedy romantic neverland already occupied by bands like Soft Cell or Fad Gadget, even though our music lacked one ounce of the archness or the theatricality of this electronic *avant garde*.

In its defence, word coupling was a popular trope of early 1980s groups. Aztec Camera did it. So did China Crisis. As did Orange Juice, Friends Again and Prefab Sprout, so we weren't so completely alone. Incidentally, these were all bands we would have killed to have been in ourselves.

However, to convey what we wanted to convey and to be as cool as the bands we were listening to, we really should have found something a lot smarter. I remember writing these two words on piles of demo tapes and home-made gig posters deep in the knowledge that we would be unlikely to 'break America' in this guise.

"Hey y'all, how's about giving a big hand for these guys who've come all the way over from good ole England just to be here tonight… er…Illicit Kiss?"

With the name sorted, sound was our next concern. How do groups find that distinctive calling card for the ears? Preferably one that sets them apart from hundreds and thousands of other hopefuls.

Work with Phil Spector, Trevor Horn or Rick Rubin, and it's the producer who holds all the cards. At other times, it's the musicians who, among themselves, manage to shape it almost organically. Other factors might include having a unique style or method of playing or recording. Listen to guitarist The Edge's multi-layered delay effects on U2 recordings or James Jamerson's super fluid bass lines on early Motown records. These can be hard to reproduce and, if you did, you would be accused of wanton plagiarism.

Even the geographical origins of the music can be an influence, hence the Delta Blues, the Mersey Sound or the House Sound of Chicago. Whatever that ingredient is, every band needs it, like they need a good booking's agent.

We neither knew nor cared much for this as we eagerly plugged into our amps and sent the decibel levels flying through the manhole cover into Jubilee Place SW3, but over time a definitive Illicit Kiss sound did somehow evolve.

Guitars were decidedly jangly, an effect achieved by picking the notes, ideally with a plectrum, instead of strumming the strings frantically. I didn't have an effects pedal board handy, but I ensured the amp's reverb button was turned well up. Two guitar players make for perfect jangle pop, think of the intro to *Mr Tambourine Man* by The Byrds or *Days* by Television. In a studio setting, double or even treble tracking the guitarist's rhythm part, with an element of delay on each, certainly does the trick.

Although I couldn't really play them, long guitar solos were a no-no. If there really was space for one in the song it would be an anti-rock statement like the two-note solo in *Boredom* by the Buzzcocks. Mine always seemed to sparkle briefly before fading out apologetically somewhere towards the end. Job done.

Drums had to avoid similar trappings of being too rock and roll. For Rory, who bizarrely admitted he would rather be in a band *without* drums, this was hardly an issue. In our twee sounding band, you could almost certainly get away without the pounding drum rolls or apocalyptic cymbal crashes.

The unsung hero of the band, bass, had to be solid and not too much of a show off. The very worst kind of bassist would try to impress with slappy high-fretted grooves borrowed from Level 42 or the funky breakdown from Rose Royce's *Car Wash*. Yawn! I lost count of how many times I heard someone sound checking their gear with the bass riff for *Another One Bites The Dust*. In our outfit, we preferred the more laid-back jazz bass leanings as heard on records by Everything But The Girl, Working Week or The Pale Fountains. We didn't have one, but a proper upright double bass would have been perfect for the job.

When it came to our vocal sound, we had Gavin's strangely pure and high-pitched singing. He was a confident front man and, unusually for a singer, would help fetch the gear from the back of the car. His voice, however, was more Aled than Tom Jones. Its tone and timbre were as far away from Tom Waits, Robert Plant or Bon Scott from AC/DC as was humanly possible.

Again, there was nothing inherently wrong with this, as we all appreciated the winsome English soundscape of Dream Academy's *Life In A Northern Town* or *First Picture Of You* by The Lotus Eaters.

It was *the* moment, after all, for sensitive boys who carried around large semi-acoustic guitars and wore clean white shirts with a Bowie-goes-to-Berlin haircut.

'A band who mixes the romanticism of stolen promises and broken hearts à la *Gone With The Wind,*' wrote one of our ecstatic reviewers. 'Their song *Seasons* was the best of the night. More like that and we could be hearing from them on vinyl pretty soon!'

Today you might describe this kind of music as sophisiti-pop, a niche musical subgenre that flourished briefly in the 1980s and which borrowed largely from soft rock, old Hollywood film scores and Latin jazz. Back then this sound didn't really have a name, but it sure wasn't rock and roll.

I'm not sure what the others were thinking, but my perfect pop star combined elements of Lloyd Cole (good hair, long words), Edwyn Collins (good hair, Ray-Ban Wayfarers, stripey t-shirts), Martin Fry (long words, lamé and lexicons) plus helpings of effortless cool and sophistication from Sade. Although this was the mid-1980s, a time when British-made pop was fast becoming one of our greatest exports, particularly in the US which had Duran Duran and Billy Idol on an MTV* loop, the last thing I wanted was for us to look or sound like Nik Kershaw, Go West or Howard Jones.

These more polished and successful acts, along with the likes of A-ha, Flock of Seagulls and Kajagoogoo, really led the field commercially, incorporating the latest developments in recording technology to project their all-conquering chart missiles. Image-wise, however, they were a fashion crime scene in an assortment of padded shoulders, two tone mullets and appalling gap year jewellery.

In contrast, we stuck rigidly to what was becoming a standard indie boy band look of bold quiffs and floppy fringes. We wore garish paisley shirts or plain polo necks with ill-fitting pleated thrift store trousers twinned with leather sandals. Our wardrobes were almost entirely vintage, as were our instruments, as indeed was our whole approach to writing, playing and recording music.

*The US-based cable television channel Music Television launched in 1981.

So, while the Art of Noise and Peter Gabriel tinkered with their Fairlight samples and The Human League's producer got busy programming the commercial catnip of electronic Linn drums, I was tearing my hair out over botched song endings in a smoke-filled former coal cellar. My vintage Burns 'Sonic' electric guitar feeding back horribly from the ancient British valve amp in the corner only added to the Luddite vibe.

Although we had no shortage of lyrics or basic melodies to bring to rehearsals, and we generally worked on songs with beginnings, middles and ends, the attraction for me was to find those rare and exquisite combinations of drums, bass and guitar.

Rob, Rory and I would occasionally reach these moments that were the musical equivalents of tantric sex or flying serenely over the clouds.

"Ooh, that does sound a bit Teardrop Explodes!" we would all nod appreciably to each other.

"Hmm, this riff has a nice Killing Joke vibe to it, let's keep this going just a few more minutes."

Here in this tiny basement, we imagined we were breaking free from the constraints of bosses and band leaders or, indeed, any formal artistic direction. These uncharted sonic journeys eventually ran out of steam, of course, but without such experimentation – or 'jamming' as we call it in the trade – there was really no fun in being in bands.

"Turn it down!" protested Gavin, putting his fingers in his ears.

We would carry on regardless, smirking to each other as Gavin shuffled his lyric sheets on his lap hoping that we'd return to our senses and go back to the start. Such flashes of inspiration could be lost forever if someone failed to press the record button on our tape recorder.

You wouldn't know it by listening to them, but some of our songs took literally hours and hours of rehearsal time and we more than broke the 10,000 hour principle.* In hindsight, we could have saved

*Academic research publicised in Malcolm Gladwell's book *Outliers* (2008) which supports the theory that to achieve excellence in any chosen field (playing the violin, becoming a chess master or basketball star etc.) requires at least 10,000 hours of practice.

ourselves the bother by taking a cue from the Human League and programming a portable synthesizer at home, then inviting some competent session musicians in towards the end. It would certainly have saved us on broken guitar strings and damaged egos.

And as we began to chip away at those 10,000 hours and round off those rougher edges by playing the so-called London 'toilet circuit' of pubs, clubs and independent music venues, we decided it was time for a name change.

Several ideas were thrown into the hat including Sunshine Sunday, Indigo Mood, Fortune and One Million Faces, but the one we eventually settled on appeared to us in bright lights as Rob's car sped past the Notting Hill Coronet cinema late one Saturday night. "Stranger Than Paradise. That's it!" I slurred from somewhere in the back, twisting my head around to catch the full effect of our chance discovery.

"We're not strange, we're normal," argued Rob, putting his foot down all the way to Marble Arch. "Who wants to see a band that describes themselves as *strange*?"

"Yeah, it sounds a bit of a mouthful. Not at all catchy," added Gavin.

"Well, Frankie Goes To Hollywood is a bit of a mouthful too," I countered, "but that didn't stop them getting to number one."

"Suppose so," admitted our singer.

"And Curiosity Killed The Cat. And that new lot Johnny Hates Jazz. They don't have short catchy names."

Consequently, with our new name, a shameless lift from the briefly hip Jim Jarmusch movie playing at a run-down repertory cinema famous for screening such cult gems as *Night of the Living Dead* and *The Texas Chainsaw Massacre*, we entered our second phase. Well, if Bowie and Madonna could re-invent themselves over and over again, why couldn't we?

Resolving to play the pop game properly this time and alert the press and the record companies to our not so obvious talent, the new improved Stranger Than Paradise ditched the lost indie boy look and agreed to write some tunes that people might actually listen to.

I asked an ex-flatmate if he could take some professional photos of us. First there was the shoot with our faces lit up like matinee idols dressed in preppy club blazers, ties and polo necks. Sometime after that, we adopted a back-to-basics Beastie Boys-style hip hop guise. Our photographer mate captured us dancing self-consciously in a circle in our MA-1 US air force bomber jackets and baseball hats. Neither, I'm afraid, got us onto the front pages of *Smash Hits*.

However, we were undoubtedly in the right place at the right time for a shot at pop super stardom, and it was true that record companies were throwing insane amounts of money at unsigned acts. The gossip doing the rounds about The Roaring Boys was a case in point. Signed by Epic for an extraordinary six-figure deal, the much-hyped Cambridge-based Duran Duran-a-likes failed to even dent the Top 40 with their debut single *Every Second of the Day*, becoming a byword for the era's record industry excess.

But seeing it from our humble position, attracting the interest of a major or even an independent label felt like scaling Everest. It would require an almost superhuman tenacity just to get to base camp and, even after that, there was no guarantee we would make it to the summit.

And unlike with today's highly atomised music industry, there was always the proverbial 'gatekeeper' to deter the untalented, the aged, the difficult to handle or just the plain old ugly. The term gatekeeper could refer to any number of powerful individuals or organisations, notably the BBC and commercial broadcasters, as well as the music press, high street retailers, concert promoters and ultimately the audience.

This huge, daunting monolith had been in place since time immemorial. These were the people, after all, who had rejected the first demo by The Beatles; the people who had sheltered for decades the paedophile disc jockey turned television presenter Jimmy Savile; the people who would one day green light the Spice Girls movie *Spice World*.

But like the Berlin Wall, which would eventually turn to rubble, the monolith wasn't completely indestructible. We had proof of this after a musician friend of ours had stalked the DJ, John Peel, outside Broadcasting House with his band's hastily recorded demo tape. This was the same friend who only a few years earlier had drummed briefly in Small Print and joined the Thompson Twins on stage at The Marquee, pinching a cowbell and some cheap vocal microphones off them in the process.

Peel, the legendary late-night jock known for his eccentric but, on the whole, sound musical tastes had, to my friend's surprise, rewarded him and his band by inviting them on for a live session. I tried to pull off something similar outside the Portland Place entrance to Radio 1. Hoping to find Peel or, failing that, the near credible David 'Kid' Jensen, I could only find Simon Bates, famous for his soppy but phenomenally successful 'Our Tune' segment.

"Sorry guys, no more tapes," came the inevitable brush off from this housewives' favourite with his trademark big wire framed glasses, "you see, we're absolutely chokka right now!"

I had failed in this attempt at shameless self-promotion but, luckily for us, our own front man, Gavin, had all the qualities needed to meet industry types face to face. He even wrote down the names of all the current A&R's* listed in a leather-bound contacts book. He didn't even mind being kept on hold by their secretaries during his one-hour lunch break at his office in The Strand.

One of these contacts, a former Radio 1 disc jockey who had interviewed The Beatles and had produced smash hit records for Gary Glitter and the Bay City Rollers, asked us if we would visit him so he could hear our latest tunes.

Having picked up Gavin in Grannie Squirrel's beige Austin Allegro (grannie had been banned from driving so the Allegro became my first car) we then drove up the M1 motorway turning off at a junction shortly before Northampton.

I didn't really know what a former Radio 1 DJ's home would look like, but this certainly wasn't it. We parked up in the drive and knocked on the front door waiting several minutes before a balding, unshaven man in tracksuit bottoms appeared.

"Hi," said Gavin, "are you by any chance Chris?"

*Artists and repertoire (also known as the 'umms and ahhs'), the department of a record company responsible for discovering and developing up-and-coming artists and songwriters.

"Er...yes, that's me. Come in."

It was a big untidy house with several rooms leading off a sizeable hallway.

"Excuse my mother," said the former pop jock pointing to an old woman crumpled in an armchair. "She's got dementia and can be a bit of a pain to be honest."

"Oh, okay," I tried to answer sympathetically.

"ARE..YOU...AL...RIGHT, MO-THER?"

It took a few moments for the old lady to stir but very soon she was nodding away to the sound of her son's voice. A dog barked angrily in another part of the house.

"So, here we are!" announced the ex-DJ, leading us into what looked like a disused garage.

There was a dusty worktable with a mono record player on top and piles of singles without their covers strewn all over place. On the wall was a framed black and white photograph of him posing with a group of familiar Radio 1 stars outside Broadcasting House in 1967. My god, he had let himself go since then.

"Right," he said, grabbing a pile of old singles, "I'm going to play you an absolutely marvellous song that I produced for the Rollers back in '71."

The room was draughty. I edged closer to Gavin for some reassurance. As the music played, the DJ closed his eyes and seemed to go into some sort of trance but then he abruptly took the needle off.

"I'm so dreadfully sorry, I forgot to offer you some tea. You know, I could do with a couple of young musicians like you around the house. You see, I've got so many great ideas but nobody to help me record them in the studio."

From what I had seen or heard so far there didn't seem to be much common ground between us. A collaboration with this madman seemed absurd.

"It's getting dark. Shouldn't we be heading back to London?" I nudged Gavin, picking up on the increasingly creepy vibe.

"But you could stay here for a while," he offered, as our feet crunched the stones on his driveway. "I have a couple of spare rooms free. Why don't you both have a think about it?"

The engine of the Allegro started up. The big house and its gravel driveway quickly vanished from the rear-view mirror.

Our decision to bolt turned out to be a sensible one. Only a year later the former Radio 1 man was imprisoned for gross indecency with a minor. Among a litany of other criminal charges, he was later caught running a large paedophile ring in Prague and served five years in a Slovakian jail for publishing child pornography. A High Court judge described him as "utterly depraved".

Rather more promisingly, the band's second gig was at the Rock Garden in Covent Garden where a good-looking young man with a ponytail introduced himself to us while we were changing backstage.

"Hi, I'm Joe," he said, squeezing past the support band Bandits At 4 O' Clock who each had a colourful kamikaze style headband on.

"Hey, Joe, where are you going with that gun in your hand?" I couldn't resist it.

He laughed.

"I'm from EMI. I've come to check out The Illicit Kiss. Is that you?"

"Yeah, that's us!" I replied.

In contrast to creepy Chris, Joe seemed nice and normal and was about the same age as us.

"Cigarette?"

"Sure," I said taking one of his Marlboro Reds straight from the packet.

As we had already wrapped up our soundcheck, I invited him for a stroll and a smoke outside in the Piazza.

I filled Joe in about the band's story and how, in only a short space of time, we had written twelve good songs ranging from the instant pop/soul of *Will You Remember?* to *Chance Would Be A Fine Thing*, a socially conscious number about poverty and dashed aspirations with a hard driving rockabilly beat; an idea I nicked from The Smiths.

"I reckon we'll soon have enough material for an album," I announced boldly as we said goodbye outside the club's entrance.

"Yeah. Well, good luck, I'll see you later," he said, handing me his card. "And if we don't catch each other afterwards, be sure to ring the office."

So it was that a few weeks later I found myself on the inside of EMI House. The very same West End office block where those clean-cut Beatles had famously grinned down at photographer Angus McBean from its modernist glass and concrete stairwell.

Dressed in a bright red vintage shirt with cowboy style collar tips bought from the King's Road and clutching our newly recorded demo cassette, with a home-made cover I had designed myself using a sheet of Letraset, I entered the same A&R man's office.

It was just as I imagined it would be. In one corner was an enormous state-of-the-art music centre which had giant matt black speakers on either side. Piles of fresh vinyl records, still in their cellophane wrappers, littered the floor area around us.

In his executive leather chair set behind an enormous white desk Joe was looking strangely moody and just a little intense. Still, he managed to shake my outstretched right hand.

"Er, Dan, hello. How's it going?" he mumbled.

"Great. I've brought our new demo along with me. We're really pleased with it!"

"Right, okay…er, then I guess we'd better have a listen."

Joe seemed a little less effusive than he had been at the Rock Garden. I wondered if I had done something to upset him.

After handing him the tape, I collapsed into a deep light brown sofa opposite the impressive in-house sound system. I marvelled at the tour posters and signed gold discs – ones by Kate Bush, Pet Shop Boys, Talk Talk and other best-selling EMI artists – that covered the vast wall surface of this Manchester Square headquarters.

Just as he had done backstage at the Rock Garden, Joe offered me a Marlboro – a positive omen at last – taking one for himself before pressing the play button.

Now the familiar sound of my jingly jangly semi-acoustic guitar rang out all over the room. Gosh, the studio's double tracking and my infectious sliding lead line was sounding great. I was liking this bit a lot. So, this is the moment everything changes! I dared wonder as Rory's snare drum cracked into action and then Rob's probing bass joined in.

'Don't let me go, don't let me go tonight', crooned Gavin convincingly.

Looking across the room for signs of approval I could see Joe drumming his fingers on the big white desk in front of him. Maybe those misspent years weren't so wasted after all?

The next track *The Boy Inside* had a cool jazzy Doors vibe. Joe was going to love this one too. Failing that there was the one called *Seasons* which sounded a lot like The Velvet Underground.

In my mind, I had already passed 'Go' and collected my £200. I had ripped open my Wonka chocolate bar and waved aloft my Golden Ticket.

I hadn't got as far as spending the entirety of EMI's substantial advance, but I may just have been thinking about putting a deposit down on that metallic blue Karmann Ghia I had seen advertised in *Loot*. I would almost certainly be getting the hell out of Clapham North with its dreary, wood-chipped hallway, nicotine-stained ceilings and revolting flowery curtains.

We were halfway through track three, a sort of bossa nova-ish love song called *What Went Wrong*, which would have sounded amazing in a Covent Garden wine bar, but then Joe leant over and pressed the pause button.

"Er, so…what do you reckon, Joe?" I asked, putting an end to the dreadful silence.

"Um, yeah, well, it's alright," said the A&R man somewhat doubtfully.

"You mean to say you liked some of the tracks?"

I could hear another A&R man on the phone in the adjoining room. Something about being on the guest list for a show that night at The Fridge in Brixton.

"Yeah…I liked it, the songs are alright. I mean, you've got *potential*."

Potential. I liked that word. But it wasn't the same as "sign along the dotted line with EMI tomorrow".

"The thing is, Dan, and try not to take this too badly, we're looking for something different. Something a bit edgier. Something darker. You know…a bit like the next Killing Joke. Anything but the old Haircut 100!"

I could see exactly what he meant.

"Very well, Joe. In that case we'll get rid of our all too eager to please, boy-next-door style singer. We'll write some doom-laden songs about war and pestilence and then we'll bring you another tape in a few weeks. How does that sound?"

This *should* have been the immediate come back. Not my pathetic "Oh."

In a matter of minutes, I had handed back my pass to the uniformed guard at reception and was now standing on the pavement outside wondering what indeed *had* gone wrong.

Ah well, there were several more A&R's on Gavin's list: Colin Bell at London, Jeff Chegwin at RCA, not forgetting Ronnie Gurr over at Virgin. Besides, didn't Manchester Square execs have serious doubts about releasing Queen's monster smash *Bohemian Rhapsody* only a decade earlier? I suppose nobody's perfect.

12.

MAKE IT BIG

Becoming the 'Next Big Thing' isn't all about talent, musicianship or having God-given star appeal. It isn't just about your manager having a bulging Filofax of top industry names. Nor is it about being booked to play endless gigs in windowless dives to a handful of loyal friends plus the odd confused-looking German tourist.

Seemingly wise to this, the KLF famously burnt £1 million of their own cash on the remote Scottish island of Jura. One million pounds gone, just like that. The Red Hot Chilli Peppers even went to the lengths of putting socks on their cocks. A decade earlier, guitar pop hopefuls Stranger Than Paradise were causing media mayhem with their own series of daring, self-generated publicity stunts.

The band had willingly pulled on *Just Seventeen* t-shirts for a photo shoot with the said teen title. We had also been photographed with members of Wham! and Bananarama at a *Number One* magazine party and secured valuable column inches in the *Mail on Sunday's* colour supplement. They ran an illustrated feature story on us playing at every station on London's Circle Line, ending with a prime Saturday night performance at Buzby's nightclub on the Charing Cross Road.

Seeing an even bigger prize, Gavin suggested that we gate crash the Brit Awards at London's Grosvenor House Hotel. The event was to be hosted by Jonathan King and promised performances by Chris de Burgh, Whitney Houston and the latest 'Next Big Thing' Curiosity Killed The Cat. Curiosity, who had supported us at a low-key West End club gig only a year earlier, were now flying high in the charts with their single *Down To Earth*. The jammy bastards!

Ligging, or the art of attending social functions that served *canapés* and free booze, meant you could meet your musical heroes face to face. For the fame hungry Stranger Than Paradise, this entailed fooling an army of useless West End club doormen who eased their rope barriers and allowed us into the inner sanctum of contemporary chart pop.

Several notable (and surprisingly credible) stars of the day were photographed holding up our distinctive band t-shirt. These included Neil and Chris from Pet Shop Boys, Alison Moyet of Yazoo and someone from Wet Wet Wet. Shirlie from Wham! even gave bassist Rob a cuddle at the *Number One* magazine party. We were deservedly named 'Ligger of the Night' in their post party roll of shame.

Indeed, such was our desperation to please pop's gatekeepers, and in turn be saved further years of pointless gigging, that a plan for the Brit Awards really began to take shape.

"We'll all dress up in our smartest suits and hand out our demos and band t-shirts," enthused Gavin, after one especially taxing post-work rehearsal.

"Hang on!" I protested, shooting the idea down in flames with a steely Clint Eastwood stare, "we'll never get in." "Besides," I added, "don't you find the idea of handing trophies out to pop stars faintly absurd?"

Gavin looked at me as if I had gone mad. I hadn't finished yet.

"Surely the viewers at home would readily trade their miserable lives for the ones led by those preening show ponies up there on stage? What do *they* need awards for?"

No one seemed interested in my argument.

"Anyway, I'm just not coming. Good luck to you."

Despite my serious reservations, I wished Gavin and Rob all the best in their foolhardy smash and grab.

"Be sure to abuse the free *canapés!* Have a glass or two of Krug for me!"

Imagine my surprise, therefore, when the following words were uttered by daytime Radio 1 jock Peter Powell only a few days later. Remember that in its 1980s heyday the nation's number one pop station was commanding audiences of over 20 million listeners weekly:

"You saw the Brit Awards on the telly so there's no point in me talking about that side of it. What I will say is that the best bit of the entire evening was when a young band had blagged their way past security and past everybody else and came up to as many tables as they could find with media people on and put in their hands a tape. The young man who came up to me who fronted the band Stranger Than Paradise said: 'You may never listen to this, but I thought I'd try to get into this occasion and find as many people as I can who can possibly help us.' And for that, ten out of ten. Stranger Than Paradise, good luck to you."

Oh, so there was a god, after all!

The prime-time DJ and regular *Top of the Pops* presenter may well have called us the 'best bit of the entire evening' live on the air but I wonder if Bob Geldof agreed with the sentiment as our bass player handed his wife, Paula Yates, one of our cassettes suggesting she might want to hear a "really good band", as opposed presumably to The Boomtown Rats.

And how did such guerilla marketing tactics sit, I wonder, with *Bat Out of Hell* singer Meatloaf as Gavin and Rob stuck Stranger Than Paradise promo stickers on him while MTV attempted to conduct a live interview?

Still, priceless publicity such as this was worth at least a dozen gigs on the so-called 'toilet circuit', a depressing ritual of now long closed-down pubs in Harlesden, Hammersmith, Camden, Kentish Town and other scruffy inner London hubs.

Understandably, the London pub scene would have been a turn off for Madonna or Tears For Fears but, over time, we found it a valuable learning curve, helping us to decide which of our songs clicked with audiences and which ones didn't.

The songs you encored with were usually the ones that audience members reacted to most positively. If they danced or even nodded their heads in time to the music you were on the right track. Encores, of course, are a live performance ritual that should never be taken for granted.

Indeed, sometimes we didn't even make it to the end. At the Half Moon pub in Herne Hill we were told to finish our set early, possibly due to the fact that I had taken over on lead vocal duties after Gavin was struck down by laryngitis at the very last minute. In a repeat of the school triangle band fiasco, aged eight, I simply froze when it came to delivering my lines. Or maybe I just forgot them.

"You'll never play here again," said the promoter prophetically when I went over to remonstrate with the sound guy, who had literally pulled the plug on us.

There were moments, however, when each performance could have been a portal to a brave new world of limos, model girlfriends and unlimited free studio time, with us nervously checking the guest list in case someone from Virgin or CBS was in the house.

We were asked to appear at a raucous Australia Day celebration for *TNT* magazine with the band perched high up on a revolving stage at the Empire Ballroom in Leicester Square.

At times, the steady chants of *Waltzing Matilda* threatened to drown out our funky guitar pop, augmented this time by a conga player and our feisty new backing singer, Emma, resplendent in high heels and fishnet stockings. I have never seen so many drunks in one room together, not even at Munich's *Oktoberfest,* nor at the San Fermin festival in Pamplona.

Then, after a leading promoter likened our song *Secret Love* to something off the Sade album, we appeared on a jazz revival bill at the iconic Astoria on the Charing Cross Road, coming on after a dazzling display of bebop dancing from the IDJ crew. My friend, Gary, still wearing his French raincoat, studiously smoked a pipe in the wings.

We even managed to command the stage at Ronnie Scott's jazz club, thereby impressing our parents into the bargain. Ronnie's is an institution which had previously hosted Duke Ellington, Nina Simone and hundreds of other jazz and blues greats. I still wonder what the audience made of our decidedly cheesy version of Van

Morrison's *Moondance.* Star spotter Gavin didn't seem to mind. He had a chat afterwards with the snooker player Steve Davis and asked his childhood hero, Donny Osmond, who was also in the audience, to sign an autograph.

At times, our gigs were organised with the sole purpose of showcasing our undeniable talent to record industry executives. This was undoubtedly the case when we were primed backstage at Zeeta's in Putney for the arrival of a Bertelsmann Music Group (BMG) big wig and his contact who had flown over especially from Germany. Rob must have smooth talked someone he had met at the Brit Awards.

Zeeta's, which was run by the larger-than-life Mark Fuller, formerly of The Embassy Club in Mayfair, was an anomaly on the live music scene with its Art Deco interior and its dinner-dancing vibe with liveried waiters, an exotic fish tank and clean white tablecloths. In another era, you might have expected to see Edward and Mrs Simpson swan in for a quick pre-dinner cocktail. The perfect setting, you would have thought, for an ambitious young band to meet their destiny.

After a previous appearance at the club, I was allowed in the following night to retrieve my lost leather jacket. "Come on in!" said the ebullient club promoter with a wink, "it's fetish night, but you're okay to stick around for a couple of drinks."

Which I did.

Our soundcheck at Zeeta's had gone smoothly enough, despite the in-house sound engineer being somewhat irritable and possibly a little worse for wear as he attacked various knobs on his mixing desk.

And, as we sauntered on stage in our carefully co-ordinated black and white stage gear, the omens were good. The mix coming out from the stage monitors at our feet wasn't entirely satisfactory, but our playing was unusually tight and the stage moves seemed right. Meanwhile our newly recruited keyboard player, Bert, who came from a family of professional musicians, was adding the required shine which always seemed to be absent from our live shows.

Towards the end of our set, two stunningly tall female fans joined us on stage for our final number, a funky dance groove with an interminable sax solo we called *Shake, Shake!*

Looking over hopefully to the white-clothed dinner table where our friends from BMG were sitting, I could see there were now two empty chairs. Where on earth had they disappeared to?

Over by the bar, Zeeta's irascible sound engineer was practically slumped over his mixing desk while several empty pint glasses teetered on the edge of it. Had we been thwarted at the last hurdle by the God of Dire Stage Sound? Lord knows! We never heard from BMG again.

Just a few weeks later, we were caught out equally unawares at an illegal warehouse party we had agreed to play at under the railway arches of London Bridge. Getting paid or being signed by a major label wasn't the draw of this unusual booking, more the fact that the promoter seemed to have invited half of London to this cavernous space for a rave that was expected to go on till dawn.

This time, it wasn't just the sound engineer who was at fault. The problem was more fundamental than that. The power connected to the mixing desk, the PA system and all our stage amplifiers came not from a reliable mains supply but a small portable generator which, right from the word go, emitted a strong whiff of petrol fumes.

Whenever the entire band struck up during our sound check, the LED lights on the mixing desk would simply cut out, as if someone had pulled the plug on us.

This unfortunate pattern repeated itself several times over during our sound check that never was. At one point the pragmatic Rob even dashed to his car to syphon out more fuel for the fucked generator.

Meanwhile, the promoter had by now let in several hundred party goers who wasted no time at all in shaking their stuff to some funky rare groove classics coming from some speakers somewhere else in the building.

"I'm beginning to feel slightly dizzy," I confided to Rob as we aborted the show and planned our escapes.

My chest tightened and my eyes started to sting owing to the now visible cloud of noxious fumes hanging in the air. To the sound of *I Believe In Miracles* by the Jackson Sisters I grabbed my guitar and amplifier and headed through the poisonous fog towards the exit.

Escaping into the relatively pure and uncontaminated atmosphere of Tooley Street I saw a posse of police officers rush into the building. Armies of men in blue carrying truncheons or chunky hand torches.

With them were two or three huge Alsatian dogs who gnashed their canines, straining at their leashes to get at the growing throng of revellers. It was like a scene from the miner's strike of four years earlier but with young ravers instead of striking pit men.

When I eventually got home, I slept for over 15 hours.

Quite possibly, I was lucky to wake up at all.

13.

WHAT HAVE I DONE TO DESERVE THIS?

"Am I in hell?"

The clock on the wall ticked by slowly.

"I said, AM I IN HELL?"

Admittedly, my judgment was far from reliable, but I could make out that the person in front of me was a doctor. I suppose the white coat was a bit of a giveaway.

My heart still thumped away at a frightening pace, as fast as it was when I had witnessed my own death in the ambulance.

Terrified of what might happen next, I managed to push myself to the furthest reaches of the treatment couch.

Maxine continued to hold my hand. There were tears in her eyes as she did so.

"Am I in hell, doctor?"

This time my voice was softer and a bit croakier, but no less insistent.

Someone had to explain this mysterious turn of events to me.

The doctor looked at me in an inquisitive but slightly detached way. It made me feel like a fossil in the hands of a palaeontologist.

"Your name please?"

"No!"

"Why not?"

"Because…well, because you're the d..d..*devil*! You're the bloody *devil*, aren't you?" I cried, retreating even further back into the blue plastic covered couch. I didn't really want to ask this question in case it was answered in the affirmative.

The doctor simply ignored me. Instead, he seemed to be whispering to a tall black man with a pointy beard. The man had entered the room looking like one of the three wise men as depicted on a stained-glass window. He seemed like a godly man, perhaps even someone I could trust, but then something about his aura changed and I shuddered in his presence. Perhaps he was a devil too.

"Don't. Bloody. Touch me!"

My whirling mind carousel replayed all those evil thoughts and all those evil deeds I had committed in my all too short life. If only I had been a better person. If only I hadn't let people down.

Images of dreadful gargoyles and horned beasts came and went. Some lingered far too long for my liking. Where had they come from? How on earth was I going to stop them? I *had* to stop them!

The doctor nodded to someone else and then half a dozen more orderlies in white coats, including a hefty nurse with a rough bedside manner, rushed in to grab various parts of my body.

"You be quiet! There, you see. You *can* be a good boy."

They now had me pinned down so effectively I could no longer kick out at or punch the visible or invisible demons around me.

"Let go of me…*please*!"

The strong Dutch nurse turned me onto my side and someone pulled my jeans down. I could only watch helplessly as the devil came towards me with a terrifyingly long needle.

"Arghhhhhh!"

"There, this will help you to calm down," he hissed. "Now you will have a very deep sleep."

As my limbs lost their fight and my febrile mind began to zone out, I could hear him talking to Maxine, pretty as ever and still made up for a night out that never was.

"You're a good girl," I could hear his reverberating voice say to her. "But you should get rid of this guy. Find yourself a nice boy from Amsterdam instead!"

The getaway had started promisingly enough. There was a morning ferry crossing from Harwich followed by a slow train ride across featureless expanse of northern Holland before we finally arrived at Central Station.

On what was only our second evening, I had wandered out of the hostel on my own.

"See you in an hour!" I called out to Maxine, as she luxuriated in the hostel's avocado-coloured bath.

Later we would be eating at the Indonesian restaurant that I had spied earlier on, just off the Leidseplein. We had been dating for almost a year after she, the sulky looking brunette on the sofa, threw her arms around me as I DJ'd at a friend's birthday party. I was so happy now I could have performed a traditional Dutch clog dance. I could have been persuaded to swallow a plate of raw North Sea herrings.

Temptation is a funny thing, but alongside the Amstel canal I came across a food stall that had a handwritten menu board propped up beside it. It was manned by a chubby softly spoken hippie who wore a plain black apron. His round John Lennon spectacles made him look like a kind of psychedelic Santa Claus.

"Hey, you wanna try some really great Space Cake?"

"Sure, how much?"

Evidently the dude lived full time on the scruffy canal boat moored behind him. Piles of straw covered the deck, while a pair of chickens picked their way through some random flowerpots on the roof. As a side hustle the happy hippie was selling hash brownies, weed infused milkshakes and other stoner-ish snacks aimed, presumably, at punters just like me.

In fact, my friend, Julian, had bought a similar-looking cake from the very same spot the summer before. Without even asking what the magic ingredients were, he ate it right there and then, spending the rest of the afternoon trailing behind us with a beatific smile frozen to his pallid, sun-starved face. Later that afternoon he danced uninhibitedly to the all-female reggae act Amazulu in the Vondelpark. I figured I had nothing to be afraid of.

I handed the hippie some coins and accepted the homemade offering which came wrapped in cellophane. In my hand, the portion looked almost comically super-sized. I could have shared it among three or four fellow tourists, but it was just me by the side of the canal while my girlfriend, oblivious to the transaction, was getting ready to hit the town just a few blocks away.

Rising to the challenge, I began putting lumps of the damp sponge base into my mouth, washing each one down with gulps of cranberry juice. There was really nothing remarkable about the taste. No extract of moon crater and definitely no space dust sprinkled on top.

I celebrated the disappearance of the very last piece with a loud burp, safe in the knowledge that a marvellously mellow time was just around the corner.

To kill some more time, I paced around the block with its cute gabled houses and anarchic clusters of bicycles at every corner. I popped into a small record shop that had gig posters for the Melkweg and the Paradiso in the window. I bought some old soul records including *Float On* (*'Cancer, and my name is Larry...'*) and a rare 12-inch version of the 1974 disco smash *Rock Your Baby* by George McRae for a couple of guilders each. I then leafed through a rack of vintage cowboy shirts outside a neighbourhood thrift shop. It was still only March, but the slowly setting sun had an uplifting warmth to it.

Returning to our cosy hostel room located up a couple of flights of stairs, I could see Maxine had changed into one of her outfits. She looked gorgeous. Too good for me by half.

"Where have you been, honey?"

"Oh, I just went for a walk to the canal. Found this great little record shop. Look!"

I passed her the striped paper bag out of which my latest vinyl acquisitions peeked out.

"Guess I should have a shower myself," I said, stepping into the bathroom.

I had begun to feel a little agitated in that hostel. For some reason,

I just couldn't keep still. I had to stop myself from pacing around the edge of the bed.

"Ah, Christ!"

"What is it? Is there something wrong?" she asked, as she applied a thick coat of lip gloss to her full lips.

There was. For some reason the room seemed different. Something had changed.

"I dunno. Listen, I'm not feeling too good. I think I just need to go out and catch some fresh air."

"But, honey, you've only just got back! Why don't you lie on the bed and calm down? There's no rush."

Something about that room was indeed bothering me. It was, all of a sudden, way too small, as if it was folding in on itself. I'm not great with tight spaces at the best of times. Here, the claustrophobia was eating me away.

"I know, I know, but I've just got to get OUT!"

I put a forefinger to the side of my neck to check my pulse. It was racing so fast I could barely count the beats.

"Here, honey, have some water."

Maxine passed me a glass bottle of Evian from the bedside table. Next to it were some unwritten postcards, some loose change, a half-opened city map plus a soft packet of Peter Stuyvestant cigarettes with some Rizla papers tucked inside.

I glugged the water down hoping the coolness of it would help, but instead my chest area felt like it was burning up and my heart just kept on thumping.

Just for good measure I checked my pulse again.

"You know, I think I might be having some sort of heart attack."

Maxine had finished with her lipstick and was now trying on some circular white plastic earrings.

"I said, I think I'm having a *heart attack!*"

This stung her into action and while I continued pacing around the room wondering whether a heart could beat any faster, she zoomed downstairs to telephone for an ambulance.

Very soon there was an emergency vehicle waiting outside the hostel. A small crowd from the neighbourhood had gathered to see what the fuss was about. The whole thing felt like it had been dreamt up. Could this ambulance really be for me? Was I so seriously ill?

Ill or not, my predicament was starting to feel all so terribly real. I needed to end this far-fetched narrative by flicking a magic switch, but Maxine's anxious expression and the busy ambulance crew was a grim reminder that we were all going along with it.

"Hey, don't touch me, I'm not going!" I complained, as one of the medical team ushered me inside.

The medics settled me into a sort of comfy reclining seat. Okay, so this is where it ends. This is so unfair! What have I done to deserve *this*?

By now I was so delirious I was having several internal dialogues with myself *about* myself. It was unreal. I could also clearly look down in judgment at this poor soul from a sort of fixed aerial position, as if part of me was a fly on the wall. Was I about to witness my own demise, here in this ordinary ambulance somewhere in the back streets of Amsterdam? As Maxine continued to stroke my hand my mood veered between the downright aggressive and the tragically pitiful.

"Please, help me. I'm dying! *Please!*"

The time lapse between the moment we alighted from the ambulance and the moment the white coated doctor finally got around to seeing us in the waiting room was probably only a matter of minutes, but to me it felt like an eternity.

Life in slow motion should, in theory, throw up some interesting possibilities, but, in my case, it simply allowed my overly stimulated brain to invent a series of fanciful new scenarios, all of which were wholly unwelcome.

One of these was that the staff, including members of the ambulance crew and the hospital receptionists, were inherently evil and probably all working for some higher authority. The devil.

I told myself I would resist these demons at all costs and, if possible, take a few of them down with me before my descent into hell and damnation.

Following my sedation at the hands of the dastardly doctor and his gang, Maxine and I had no option but to shuffle out into the dark night to find a taxi back to our hostel. When we returned, we found the landlady had left our passports on a sideboard in the hallway.

"We do not like the drugs here. You must leave first thing in the morning!" she hissed at us as we climbed the staircase one last time.

I had a deep and comfortable enough sleep in the bed but, to my dismay, woke up feeling strange again. It was as if my spirit had vanished overnight. I was more than a little apprehensive. As I buttoned up my shirt, it felt as if my previous life had ended and I, a representative of the living dead, was struggling along blindly towards what could only be another terrible outcome. Purgatory?

It didn't help that we had to wait around all day for our train connection to the Hook of Holland where we would be catching the overnight sea crossing.

Given a day to spare in the centre of old Amsterdam, most people would have little trouble in finding something to do. Low slung canal tour boats waited invitingly on the Prinsengracht as would have Rembrandt's painting *The Night Watch* in the Rijksmuseum, but I was hardly fit for such endeavours. All I could manage was a painfully slow plod around the busy commercial centre, dodging the trams and the cyclists in this fearful and paranoid state, and all the time feeling unsure about which world I now inhabited.

The sights, the sounds and the smells around us seemed real and familiar enough, but around every corner lurked devils, demons and terrible, terrible witches.

An evil conspiracy was playing itself out, and it would do its best to thwart our safe passage home. My sensitivity was such that even an impromptu dance by some street puppets became a scene of dread and horror from which I immediately fled. Maxine found me cowering behind a bench on the other side of the road.

Even with her flawless face in the glorious spring sunshine, Maxine too would feel the full blast of my paranoia.

"So you're a witch too!" I railed at her, as she cradled my poor, tired head against her bosom.

"You're a *witch*, aren't you? I knew it!"

That evening, as the warm sun set all over again, Maxine somehow managed to haul us and our bags onto the safety of a waiting passenger train. By the time we reached the port, darkness had fallen. With some luck and a little ingenuity, she had found tickets and a sleeping berth on the night crossing.

Ideally the nightmare would have ended right there and then, but there was another twist in the tale.

As we reached the embarkation ramp, I spied a ticket collector from the ferry company standing just a few yards ahead of us. I began to feel jittery and unsettled all over again. "Maxine, we must turn back now! This is a trick. Please, please, we must turn back!"

Clasping my hand firmly, Maxine handed over our passports and I recoiled in disgust as the official put his wicked stamp on the pages inside mine.

"There," he said, staring at me coldly, just as the evil doctor had done the night before.

It was a cruel and definitive smile, possibly the last smile I would ever see again. Then, he finally waved us through.

"Aha, ha, ha-ha, ha ha! Velkom to HELL!"

14.

SIGN OF THE TIMES

Things were never quite the same after Amsterdam. I dragged myself up each morning to attend lectures in Regent Street but I was barely checking in. Something awful had happened to my brain and I hoped to God that nobody had clocked onto this. And, while my mind slowly found a way back through the dense and confusing fog, the 1980s suddenly decided to hit the turbo charge button.

It's hard to put a finger on when exactly this was, but let's say this was around the time Frankie said Relax, George Michael left Wham! to go solo or when Simon Le Bon bought a yacht.

A number of political and social factors were also at play, including the deregulation of City trading aka 'The Big Bang' as well as Margaret Thatcher's defeat of the striking mining unions and the subsequent pit closures. There was also a property boom fuelled by the sale of council homes, while shares for British Telecom, British Airways and other previously state-owned companies were being sold on the Stock Exchange.

Another vital sign of the times was our sudden obsession with 'style' as we switched from a manufacturing-led economy to an increasingly sales and services model. Suddenly, style became not just something that you noticed in a nightclub queue or in the pages of *The Face* or *i-D* magazine. It was fast becoming a 24-hour obsession for practically every young person between the age of 18 and 25.

What was abundantly clear about this most frenzied second act of the decade was that people suddenly seemed to have larger disposable incomes. I knew this because I worked in a Covent Garden clothes shop every Saturday. Usually, we would take over £12,000 in one day's trading. That's roughly £50,000 in today's money.

The co-owner of the business, a thirty-something clothes obsessive who, naturally, carried a Filofax, chain smoked Marlboros and had a hot mixed-race girlfriend with a New York accent, took a liking to my salmon pink buttoned-down shirt which I wore to the job interview. In his knowing nasal voice, he told me in great detail how my collars had just enough drop to create the perfect Ivy League* silhouette.

Blazer, which occupied a small premises on Long Acre just around the corner from Paul Smith's flagship store in Floral Street, sold the sort of smart workaday staples you would later find in Gap, which didn't arrive in the UK until 1987. Our best-selling items included Oxford cotton shirts, Harris tweed jackets, plain Shetland jumpers and, of course, the classic stone coloured chino trouser.

Amazingly, clothes like these were appealing to a growing clientele of West End ad men and designers (Yuppies, if you prefer) and, on Saturdays, the brickies, roofers and plasterers who carried fresh wads of twenty-pound notes in their jean pockets.

Harry Enfield's comic character Loadsamoney, who first appeared on Channel 4's *Friday Night Live*, could have been based on any one of these customers as they snapped up £300 leather aviator jackets and their favourite French designer jeans.

"Oi, what's the damage on these strides?" asked one of these newly minted tradesmen to my Polish born colleague, Marek. Unsure about the shopper's colloquial turn of phrase, Marek could only reassure him.

"Oh no, these trousers have no damage on them, they are totally brand new!"

Stuck at the coal face of style in WC2, we were an interesting cross section of youth.

*Smart sports casual look also known as 'Preppy'. The style of dressing originated in 1950s US college campuses and was later adopted by actors Paul Newman, Robert Redford and Steve McQueen.

There were the wannabe rock stars including myself and someone from the band Then Jerico, plus a few resting models, DJ's and actors, one of whom had been in the credible teen cult film *Scum* and who did passable impressions of Marlon Brando in *The Godfather*.

On top of this were the art students from nearby Central St Martin's plus a few ambitious retail careerists, some closet queens and the hardcore clubby hedonists. The latter group took a while to warm up in the morning and by mid-afternoon they were practically dead on their feet.

Surprisingly enough, we all rubbed along happily in this 1,000 square foot of prime retail space. Basically, we were there to fold jumpers, pin trousers to the correct length and help customers find the right necktie for their choice of plain blue, white or candy-striped shirt.

It seemed, however, that selling preppy gear here in revitalised Covent Garden was the next best thing to a finishing school for anyone wanting to break into the media, fashion or the arts. Indeed, one colleague from the shop floor went on to present a popular television football show while another later became the face of Channel 4's *The Big Breakfast*.

Always keen to entertain his audience (just as long as you were prepared to laugh along), the would-be broadcaster had us in stitches as he did his funny accents and imitated the most obvious physical quirks of the customers. "Look everybody, it's Midge Ure," he muttered, as a small man with pointy sideburns shuffled through the door. "It's Sting, it's Sting!" he would whisper conspiratorially, as a man in a long leather coat with spiky bleached hair inspected a pile of cotton V-necked jumpers.

On another occasion, this time a particularly busy afternoon during which long queues had formed outside in Long Acre, our star in waiting misled shoppers into our tiny stock room basement with a sign that read: 'THIS WAY FOR MORE SALE ITEMS!'

The guy in charge of the stock room nearly had a meltdown as he helplessly watched wave upon wave of customers lay waste to his orderly piles of jeans and beautifully wrapped shirts.

When it came to celebrities, it wasn't so out of the ordinary for a big household name to just walk in unannounced. Our ever-so-slightly camp cashier, Roger, nearly had a fit of the vapours when, on separate occasions, David Bowie, Terence Trent D'Arby and Rupert Everett were spotted around the corner in Floral Street. Perhaps less impressively, there were visits by 'Wicksy' from East Enders and I sold a tweed jacket to Michael Palin who, needless to say, was very nice indeed.

Members of Big Audio Dynamite, the electro/rock/hip hop off shoot of The Clash, were less easy to please.

"Hey man, you see that white mac in the window?"

It was Don Letts, aka 'Rebel Dread', the dreadlocked punk rock filmmaker who, along with his BAD sidekicks Mick Jones, Greg Roberts and Dan Donovan, came marching in one afternoon.

"Yes," I replied, thinking I had at last found some discerning customers worth knowing. I loved BAD's innovative debut album *This Is Big Audio Dynamite* with its 'made in London' guitar twang, dubby hip hop beats and cheeky samples taken from Spaghetti Westerns and the cult Nic Roeg film *Performance*.

"Right then. We're gonna need four of these," added the DJ and top video director, zoning in on our rail of knee length French Chipie macs.

These raincoats went down very well with our customers as they had an unfussy clean line and, on the inside, a distinguished tartan lining. People would remark how much they resembled the iconic waterproof coat worn by the spy Harry Palmer (played by Michael Caine) in *The Ipcress File*.

Sadly, there were only half a dozen of these garments left on the rail. Most were in navy blue and the two white ones were each in a size Small. Members of BAD would have struggled to get into these – frontman Mick Jones was almost six feet tall!

"So you're telling me you ain't got 'em, man?"

"Well, maybe we do have some somewhere. I could go downstairs and have a look for you," I suggested, trotting off in the direction of the basement.

I was only too eager to please this bunch of musicians who seemed to have total control over what they were doing. Not just with the music but with their image too. Indeed, no one had quite managed to fuse the raw energy of punk with the more contemporary New York stylings of hip hop or Jamaican reggae as they had.

"I'm sorry," I said, returning to the shop floor empty handed.

"You *wot*?" said the BAD member incredulously. "You mean to say you don't have 'em here?"

"Not here, I'm afraid. But I can call our Bond Street shop to see if they have any. If Bond Street do, I'll get someone to send them over first thing tomorrow."

He looked utterly crestfallen.

"You promise?"

"Of course."

"Yeah, well you'd better!" snarled Letts, summoning his gang together and pointing an accusatory finger at me all the way to the exit.

"We're all coming back tomorrow and if you don't have 'em, there's gonna be *big* trouble!"

Out stormed the four horsemen of the punk/hip hop apocalypse.

So, I had nearly sold some trendy raincoats to an achingly hip new band. And in this tiny backwater of the fashion world, I was receiving an education that went far beyond the skills required to placate an egotistical pop star or persuade a resting Python to part with his hard-won earnings.

Soul, reggae, funk and jazz music played on the shop's in-house cassette deck helping us to get through the long but hardly ever boring days. Of course there were the inevitable clashes of taste as we lobbied for our personal mix tapes to get an airing.

Normally our manager and Andy Warhol lookalike, Steven, had the final word on this, which meant I must have listened to Lou Reed's *Transformer*, *Little Creatures* by Talking Heads and *Swoon* by Prefab Sprout at least three thousand times during my time there. The boss occasionally made an appearance in the shop and would insist that Vivaldi's *Four Seasons* was the only way to start the day while we frantically hoovered the carpets or folded chambray shirts ready for the mid-morning assault. These invigorating 18th century violin concertos, particularly the ubiquitous *Spring*, would become the soundtrack for thousands of landline users as they waited to be put through to their utility provider or council services hotline.

On days when Steven was off sick, there was generally a free for all at the cassette deck with bemused customers being treated to *The Best of Marilyn Munroe*, *Swordfishtrombones* by Tom Waits, some Indo Jazz Fusion or even snippets of an obscure Italian movie score.

My own contribution to the in-store ambience was the *Midnight Cowboy* film soundtrack, which for some reason struck a chord with me. I must have watched this 1969 John Schlesinger classic dozens of times on VHS video and could quote it at length verbatim.

There were, indeed, some dark themes being explored but, tell me, which twenty-one-year-old wouldn't have wanted to attend the psychedelic Warhol-esque party the protagonist Joe Buck (played by Jon Voight) attends with his friend 'Ratso' Rizzo (Dustin Hoffman)? Track number two, side two, *Old Man Willow* by the New York *avant garde* rock outfit, Elephant's Memory hinted at all the things I'd missed out on by being born too late for the 1960s love in.

I'm not sure what the customers thought as they browsed twin pocketed poplin shirts or helped themselves to pairs of Argyle socks, but I was instantly drawn in by the tune's slightly menacing organ motif which develops into a *Wicker Man* style folk chant before going headlong into a free form jazz work out. I loved the bonkers walking bass lines and the wailing clarinet, followed by a tripped-out organ run, which made Ray Manzarek's solo in *Light My Fire* sound like the theme tune to *The Magic Roundabout*.*

While the *Midnight Cowboy* soundtrack undeniably won my discerning colleagues over, my cassette featuring tracks by Orange Juice, The Cure and The The got the big thumbs down, especially from the self-appointed taste makers manning our cash till. Wendy, a somewhat unpredictable young lady with ruby red lipstick and a tight black polo necked jumper, took one listen then hurled the said mix tape to its doom on the rock-hard stock room floor. Oh, rip it up and start again.

*Popular children's television programme featuring Dougal dog and pals narrated by Eric Thompson (father of actor Emma Thompson).

My new friend, Gary, the son of an English leather shoe salesman, added to the mix some exotic sounding tapes that skipped across genres as diverse as French *chanson*, 1960s beat groups and Brazilian bossa nova. We became kindred spirits as we donned our new knee-length French macs and went off to explore the delights of Soho which lay just the other side of the Charing Cross Road.

In the mid-1980s, it was still possible to savour the somewhat romanticised Soho of the 1950s. Tawdry massage parlours and seedy peep shows aside, the area still had scores of continental delis and coffee bars run by people called Toni, maintaining both their original mid-century signage and frothy cappuccinos served at chipped Formica tables.

We would dine out for around a fiver in the Pollo Bar on Old Compton Street then head for one of the Soho establishments connected to the fading demi-monde we so wished we were part of.

The French House on Dean Street with its charismatic landlord, Gaston Berlemont, sold Pernod and their beer came only in half pint measures, after a notorious incident going back to the 1920s in which a group of drunken sailors allegedly smashed pint glasses over each other's heads. And with its black and white framed photos of cyclists, pugilists and long-forgotten music hall stars, this tightly packed saloon was a magnet for the sort of characters you might have read about in a novel by Patrick Hamilton or Julian Maclaren-Ross. Some, like Francis Bacon, Lucien Freud, Jeffrey Barnard, John Hurt and barmaid Eddie McPherson (Suggs from Madness's mum) were then living and breathing examples of Soho bohemia. The trouble was that if you wanted to stop for a drink here, or at that other Soho institution The Coach and Horses around the corner in Greek Street, you had to be prepared for the regulars to be astonishingly rude to you.

Everyone wanted to be king or queen of the put down and outsiders required very thick skins indeed. You see, unlike us dilettante drinkers, the regulars had signed up for the bohemian life lock, stock and barrel. Veteran writer and broadcaster Dan Farson once brutally shoved me aside while I waited patiently for Gaston to refill my glass. "Fuck... right... off!" he boomed. On another occasion, a rather louche-looking friend of a friend simply refused my outstretched hand as we were introduced in the street outside.

"But...I could *never* shake hands with anyone who would attempt to make my acquaintance so casually," came the almost predictable barb from this pound shop Oscar Wilde.

On the other hand, rare compliments could be entirely misconstrued when in the very heart of London bohemia. My dad once introduced me to an old poet friend of his (clearly the worse for wear in the late afternoon) who turned to my dad and said rather embarrassingly: "Oh, what a lovely boy!"

"Dad," I protested later, as we walked down together towards Leicester Square, "I'm practically a thirty-year-old man, he can't be saying things like that!"

Soho was, and still is, synonymous with jazz music. Gary and I trooped off after work one evening to catch the legendary blues pianist Mose Allison playing in a tiny club off Leicester Square. We also tracked down a rare screening of *Jazz On A Summer's Day*, the colour film documentary about the 1958 Newport Jazz Festival with its impressive bill that featured Chico Hamilton and Thelonious Monk. My immersion into this somewhat idealised jazz world was well under way.

Listening to old jazz albums with their highly evocative labels by Prestige, Blue Note and Impulse! seemed like a real man's calling, requiring an ability to both concentrate through long and intricate passages of music and then make insightful comments your friends might not have considered.

Your conversation with a fellow jazz convert might end up something like this:

"Did you hear the new Miles LP?"

"Nah, the new stuff sucks!"

"So, you prefer the post be-bop Miles?"

"Yeah, I dig *Kind of Blue* and I guess *Sketches of Spain* is kinda cool."

"What about *Bitches Brew*?"

"I can't get into that."

"C'mon man, it's *Bitches Brew* with the classic Shorter/Corea/McLaughlin line up! Miles's horn playing has got some proper chops!"

Much like learning any new language, it was easy enough to get by with a few choice phrases. And by deciphering some of jazz's many codes and signposts, I managed to break down variants like 'big band', 'the cool school' or 'hard bop' against others such as 'fusion' and 'free jazz'.

I bought a pair of second-hand congas and installed them in my bedroom, playing along to old LP's by Cal Tjader and Mongo Santamaria. This more instinctive and, to my ears, infinitely less formulaic music was a long way from Stranger Than Paradise who, frankly, I was beginning to tire of.

Were we really going to make it big with our brand of lightweight jazz infected pop? Or should we finally heed the advice of EMI and go in a rockier direction, one that even post-punk posers like Spandau Ballet and ABC were now embracing? Maybe there would be room in my life for a rare groove covers band? We could play classics like *Mr Big Stuff* and *Clean Up Woman* then break into funky instrumentals from the soundtracks to *Trouble Man* and *Shaft In Africa*. Oh, and there's an easy listening revival just around the corner. Perhaps I should dust down those Sergio Mendes LP's and re-invent myself as a smooth jazz pianist. By now I was such a musical magpie that all bets were off.

Decisions, decisions. A change of scenery would surely do the trick.

15.

CRUEL SUMMER

"*Brrriiiing…*"

I stood outside the familiar looking Parisian door, figuring out what to say in my all too lapsed French.

"*Brrriiiiiiiiiiiiing,*" I pressed the buzzer on the intercom one more time.

The concierge, a stout woman wearing a utilitarian blue smock appeared. I smiled back.

"Bonjour, madame, je voudrai visiter la famille Blanchart. Est-ce possible?"

"Oui, bien sur monsieur, entrez. C'est l'appartement seize, au troisième étage."

"Ah, merci madame."

What on earth was I doing in the 15th *arrondissement* on this freezing cold spring afternoon?

I blame the magazine article I had read about the opening of Café Costes, the new Phillipe Stark designed hang out in the trendy Les Halles district. The front-page feature story focused largely on the bar's *habitués*; table upon table of gorgeous French libertines who looked exactly like Sophie Marceau or Béatrice Dalle. If this wasn't enticing enough, the bold post-modern interior was inspired by a Budapest railway station waiting room, circa 1956. There was an enormous municipal clock at one end of the bar and the dark plywood chairs had only three legs. *Three* legs, genius! *Chapeaux* off to you, Monsieur Stark!

Naturally, Gary and I bought return rail tickets to Paris. We needed to see for ourselves exactly what all the fuss was about.

Caught unawares by the coldest spring the French capital had experienced since 1914, the would-be Johnny Hallyday and his *copain* Alain Delon sought shelter in a Saint-Germain cinema, sitting through the appalling film *Highlander* starring the modish screen actor Christopher Lambert.

Realising we were only a few blocks away from the apartment where seven years earlier I had stayed during a French exchange with Frédéric – a boy who had real movie star looks – I decided to go off and surprise his family. It was an instinctive gamble but perhaps Frédéric or his parents would invite us in for a glass of *vin rouge*?

Stepping inside the warmth of the lobby with its checkerboard marble floor and dinky little service lift, the summer of 1979 came back to me as if it were yesterday.

There was that thrilling first night when I squeezed into the back of a roofless Citroen jeep alongside Fred's unfeasibly cool college friends. In the warm July air, we jumped the red lights and raced around the wide Parisian roundabouts with their enchanting, illuminated fountains. Unlike me and my boring friends, Fred's *coterie* glugged down vodka and red wine. They all smoked like chimneys and drove like maniacs.

We then decamped to the Blanchart's holiday home in the Loire-Atlantique where Fred tired of me and I lost endless games of tennis and became increasingly homesick.

Showing his cruel and unattractive side, Fred boiled some live crabs we had picked up from the rocks at a nearby beach and then thrown into a bucket of seawater.

"Leesen to ze zound of zeir screaming!" he said, turning the gas hob up for maximum effect. And when his oldest best friend came to stay, I truly became an outcast. Fred lent me his old Solex moped to ride around on, or more than likely, to get lost with.

The final straw was when his parents invited me on the family sailboat only for me to spew violently over the side as it pitched over the choppy Atlantic waves.

"He eez Nel-SON," joked Fred's father, also the skipper, much to the amusement of his sycophantic grown-up guests.

"He, he, he. Yez he eez Nel-SON. C'est drôle!" echoed one of my harshest critics as I leaned over for yet another messy regurgitation.

I found some solace with an old radio which I tuned to Radio 1 with its patchy long wave dial. One night I could just about hear the strains of *Echo Beach* by Martha and the Muffins and then a new single called *Gangsters* by The Specials. Suddenly everything had seemed alright with the world.

Now, having ascended the swirling Art Nouveau staircase, a slightly older and wiser version of myself stood outside the Blanchart's apartment. I knocked once but there was no reply. I knocked again, this time more firmly.

Assuming there must be nobody at home, I began to accept that my spontaneous visit was not to be, and so I turned around. If I had had a pen handy, I would have written them a short note and given it to the *concierge* to pass on.

Then, to my surprise, the solid apartment door creaked open and there stood an elderly woman in a dressing gown. She didn't welcome me in but instead remained there, squinting at me suspiciously.

"Madame!"

I recognised the face, but she had aged significantly since that sun-kissed August afternoon when she drove me in her blue Peugeot saloon to Nantes where I returned by train to Paris and then onto the channel ports.

"Madame, c'est moi. Daniel! Je suis venu il y a quelques années. Vous souvenez vous de moi?"

I was especially proud of myself for not falling into the trap of tutoying a middle-aged woman from the Parisian *bourgeoisie*.

I waited to be invited in but she continued to hold her ground.

"Je suis un ami de Frédéric. Souvenez-vous?"

Again, nothing.

"Je suis venu chez vous à Pornic? Vous souvenez-vous de moi?"

The door began to close.

"Vous m'avez nommé 'Nelson', vous rappelez-vous?"

The door shut with a final thud.

As I watched helplessly from the landing, I heard a cold and decidedly hostile voice mutter from the other side of the entrance.

"Nel-son? No! Je ne vous ai jamais vu!"

My rejection in Montparnasse was a reminder that the present can be less forgiving than the past, or at least the past that I had so conveniently conjured up for myself.

Returning to our favourite Soho, still shivering in our threadbare macs and without so much as a peck on the cheek from the Café Costes beauties, Gary and I found that our scruffy utopia of skin flicks and speakeasies was getting a cruel modern makeover.

Director Julien Temple's long-awaited cinematic adaptation of *Absolute Beginners* had just been released, a production in which half of the capital's club goers, models, stylists, shop assistants and all-round show-offs seemed to have had walk-on parts.

This alternative Soho was all frantic Hollywood-style choreography, neon-lit pavements and a sharp-suited David Bowie tiptoeing up and down a giant typewriter. Suddenly it seemed our Soho was a thing and, seemingly overnight, everybody else was in on the act. Give me the grim reality of the Dive Bar any night of the week.

Meanwhile the band plodded on.

We unearthed a sax player called Seamus from the Brighton-based cult swing band Ramona and the Rockets. Seamus lent our basic pop guitar sound energy, pizzazz and some laid back jazzy vibes just when we needed them most.

Perhaps we did overdo the jazz references a little and, at times, we got found out. At the upmarket Dover Street Wine Bar in Mayfair, for instance, the suave and velvet-voiced promoter had to stick both fingers in his ears as our Slade-loving drummer Jim thudded on various parts of his kit during the soundcheck. "But I thought you said you were *jazz*?" he hissed at me, as I sat there tuning my guitar.

Less successful were our attempts to find a regular keyboard player. Larry, or 'Thirsty Larry' as Rob's dad named him, stuck around for a few months and beefed up our sound no end. Larry was a graphic designer with a ponytail poking out from the back of his light blue New York Mets baseball hat. He liked to put the world to rights as he stood behind his beaten-up Casio electronic keyboard, invariably with a can of White Stripe lager on the go. On the way to rehearsals, he would demand that we stop at the nearest pub to get loaded before the session began. "Dan. Please just one, the others won't care if we're late."

People make jokes about drummers, but there should be a whole book about that most tricky of customers: the session keyboard player.

The band played some more gigs: upstairs at Ronnie Scott's, an invite only affair at The Trocadero, an all-nighter at the Rio Cinema in Dalston and then two shows at The Limelight, the fashionable new night club that occupied a former Welsh Presbyterian church on Shaftesbury Avenue. This club with its echoey sandstone galleries was rumoured to be haunted by a ghost who, it is said, disapproved of all the disreputable goings on inside. Boy George, George Michael and Grace Jones were regulars and, in this age of ecstasy, heroin and mountains of imported cocaine, several high-profile drug deaths were linked to this allegedly cursed venue.

More 'Next Big Things' crashed and burned: Yes/No People, Win, Boys Wonder, Giant, Big Pig. Why wasn't there an industry buzz about *us*?

Still, we waited for the call to come, safe in the knowledge that our increasingly polished act was an off the shelf product just waiting to fly. In fact, by this stage, we would have welcomed approaches also from Cherry Red and Rough Trade, or indeed any other of the smaller independents.

In truth, these more discerning and arguably more influential labels would have passed on a band with our sound and image. Equally, the rock critics over at the *NME* were way too busy falling over Jesus and Mary Chain, The Fall and Wedding Present to come to one of our gigs.

In contrast to these more fancied outfits, our music lacked the innovation, the edginess or the 'fuck you' attitude required to do indie rock properly. Our singer had neat, gelled hair. He smiled a lot and brought Maltesers, Aero bars and Ribena cartons with him to rehearsals. On stage he said things like "Hello, good evening and welcome!" and would cross over to the other side of the stage monitors to dance with members of the audience. Whatever the opposite of 'too cool for school' was, we were it. Any A&R person worth their salt could tell we were unlikely to rewrite the rules of rock and roll.

Apart from our increasing lack of credibility, we were also making that cardinal sin of falling 'behind the curve'. As already demonstrated by that young A&R man's reaction to our very first demo tape, it was all too easy for bands to be in this most unfortunate of places. I mean, why would anyone want to look or sound like Haircut 100 in 1985 when they could be trending like The Mission, Xmal Deutschland or The Lords of The New Church?

From our early roots channelling the made-in-Scotland, melodic soft rock of Lloyd Cole, Aztec Camera and Friends Again, it is undeniable that Stranger Than Paradise jumped several bandwagons. But, in our four-year career, we never took that all-important artistic and creative leap that artists such as Kate Bush or David Byrne made at similar career junctures. Not for us a musical foray into cosmology featuring Georgian folk singers previously heard on Werner Herzog soundtracks and recorded in a yurt. Nor were we in danger of collaborating with Brian Eno to sample found sonic textures from sub-Saharan Africa or the Middle East.

In contrast, we stuck to Smiths-inspired jangle pop, Chic-style dancefloor funk, sophisti-pop and jazz lite all whilst taking copious notes from the likes of ABC, The Blow Monkeys and Swing Out Sister as they leapfrogged over us into the higher reaches of the Top 40.

My girlfriend at the time said something which crystalised the problem perfectly after I excitedly played her our new demo which we had recorded earlier that day.

Whenever you exit the studio with a version of your latest tune, the temptation is to play it over and over again until you're sick to death of it. Everybody gets to hear it, even your mum and the cat.

"What do you think?" I asked eagerly, after playing her the first of three tracks *Release Me*. I forgot to mention that the song was inspired partly by Madonna's *Lucky Star*.

"Well," she replied eventually, "it does sound very professional."

If you want to make it as an artist in the pop business, a verdict like this is the last you want to hear. Professional? Business managers, schoolteachers or surgeons – *they* need to be professional. Not rock stars.

Do you suppose when Elvis leaned into the mic and sung '*Well, since my baby left me, I found a new place to dwell…*' he was hoping people would think his song *Heartbreak Hotel* was above all 'professional'? Did Marvin Gaye write the 1971 classic *What's Going On* thinking: "You know, what the world needs right now is something really professional sounding."

Undeterred, I wrote a song called *Change* as I attempted to learn the intricate chord pattern to the intro of Sister Sledge's *Thinking of You*. Another new one, *Far Too Easy*, had a breezy West Coast feel with a soft rock chorus reminiscent of Steely Dan. Someone even commented that my guitar sound reminded them of Ernie Isley, the dude who had played the famous lick on *Summer Breeze*. So I wasn't so short of inspiration after all.

With the help of Gavin, I wrote another called *I Don't Want This Love To Last Forever* (I could have changed the words love for 'band') which we decided to pin our last hopes on. While our songwriting partnership endured, we were both firmly committed to writing 'the perfect pop song'.

In terms of song crafting, an agreed benchmark would have been the sublime *Tinseltown In The Rain* by The Blue Nile or *When Love Breaks Down* or *Cars And Girls* by Prefab Sprout, possibly even *Crocodile Cryer*, the inexplicably obscure release by Martin Stephenson and The Daintees.

There were of course the inevitable musical differences between us. I myself could easily be persuaded that The Pointer Sisters or Hall and Oates were as relevant as My Bloody Valentine or Sonic Youth. Gavin, however, took our shared love of pop music to another level. I could grudgingly accept his liking for Go West and Living In A Box, but I was absolutely horrified to hear he was now listening to Bros and Rick Astley. So *this* was the reason I had taken part in the so called 'punk wars' of the late 1970s!

How, as someone who had hung almost religiously around the Rough Trade record shop and delved into the subculture's most esoteric offerings, including *Don't Cry Your Tears* by The Delmontes or the practically unlistenable *In and Out of Fashion* EP by The Fall/ Buzzcocks' side project The Teardrops, could I be moved by a piece of garbage like *When Will I Be Famous*?

Should I, the owner of a Pere Ubu album and a veteran of shows by Stroud-based existentialist no-wavers Blurt and the post-punk industrial funk collective A Certain Ratio, even go near the appalling pop froth of *Hold Me In Your Arms*? I felt like I had been betrayed.

Creatively, however, we often managed to meet somewhere in the middle and this particular song really did seem to have something about it. From its breezy opening sax line, the track builds from a solid platform of a grown up, mid-paced rock beat in contrast to some of our earlier, more frantic efforts. And from the moment they come in, Gavin's vocals are clear and measured. It sounds like a tune you have heard before somewhere.

For once the band (including my practically non-existent guitar) are lower in the mix, giving way to Bert's dominant synth lines which place the song perfectly in this brief pop moment dominated by Stock, Aitken and Waterman, the production team responsible for hits by Rick Astley and various cast members of the Australian soap opera *Neighbours.* For some reason the wholesome looking denizens of Ramsey Street had suddenly decided they were all round entertainers. Or maybe they just came cheap.

And like any half decent pop song, *I Don't Want This Love To Last Forever* straddles the line between the musically credible and the horribly, horribly cheesy. It's fascinating how subtle variations in instrumentation or song arrangement can make all the difference. Why, for instance, are the songs *Borderline* (Madonna) and *Spinning Around* (Kylie Minogue) still irresistible to the ear, and yet *True Blue* and *Hand On Your Heart* always have, and always will, suck?

Personally, by this stage, I had given up being the monitor of good or bad taste. Let young Bert and his zeitgeisty synth do their thing.

The repeated female chorus sing back *'I'm not asking for the world'* immediately sounds trite but is not to be underestimated either. It doesn't sound like us anymore. No matter. Overall, there was more shine and polish. I detected also a sunny universal feel and a notion that this song could be played absolutely anywhere – but ideally on a

Los Angeles freeway at drive time or at a beach bar in Cannes or San Remo.

With the right manager or some support from a major label we could have flown out and performed it in front of an adoring crowd in some sultry southern European resort. But the only journey connected to this song was when the band drove in convoy along the A13 road to Canvey Island.

The estuarial Essex backwater was known for its oil refinery and dilapidated fun fair and amusement arcade, which dated back to the 1930s. In its heyday, there would have been a narrow-gauge railway, a vast boating lake and tea dances in the Art Deco-style Casino Ballroom.

Canvey Island was also the home of the popular soul and jazz funk club The Goldmine, and the place where proto punks Dr Feelgood started playing their own brand of Essex Delta blues. Where better to film your first ever pop video?

So while A-list acts like Duran Duran, Robert Palmer and Tears For Fears hired forty foot yachts, fin-tailed Cadillacs and Armani clad super models for their videos, we mooched around various Canvey landmarks in the early spring sunshine – the bandstand, the helter-skelter and the 'guess your weight' machine – while the two young directors got down to work.

We had met these creatives while sound checking at The Limelight Club where they worked as lighting engineers. "Did we want to be featured in a low budget pop video?" they asked. "Would we mind spending a Sunday on the Essex coast? And did we object to them using experimental retro Super 8mm film stock?" Well, what do you think?

One of the crew, Mark, would become a BAFTA nominated television and film director. The other, Sim, would go on to direct multiplex-friendly blockbusters such as *Shrek* and *The Chronicles of Narnia*. I hope they remember their day out with the band that was so desperate to be the 'Next Big Thing' of 1988.

Making our first pop video was all very exciting but we were unable to unleash this promotional dynamite until the in-demand Mark and Sim had edited all the film footage to the required 4 minutes and 16 seconds.

In the meantime, our live bookings were becoming increasingly erratic – one minute we were in the bowels of a top West End nightclub, the next a boozer in a remote part of South East London. Without a single or album release to support, playing live seemed pointless. There was certainly no money in it. Shamefully, we agreed to mime along to a few of our tracks at a Tony Blackburn Capital Radio event at Le Palais, the Hammersmith club once immortalised in song by The Clash but now a pretentious nightclub with a smart/casual dress code. Embarrassingly for me, the bouncers took exception to my old college friend Helen and her posse who had ventured out from their north London squat. "Nah, you lot can't come in. You've got the wrong sort of jeans on."

Then there was the notorious Tunnel Club at the Mitre Arms pub located at the southern entrance to the Blackwall Tunnel, its decaying edifice overshadowed by a huge gas holder not far from where the site of the Millennium Dome was later earmarked.

I was from Greenwich and would have hesitated to spend five minutes in such a dump, even though going there would have enabled me to witness several up-and-coming stars at their now legendary comedy nights, among them Vic Reeves, Harry Enfield, Jerry Sadowitz and Jo Brand.

The Tunnel Club's compere was a larger-than-life character called Malcolm Hardee who wore thick National Health specs and actively encouraged the heckling of new acts. "I'd fuck her," was one of his catchphrases, and he had famously urinated on an unfortunate punter who had fallen asleep during his act.

I got into the spirit of this anarchic south London venue by wearing a straw cowboy hat and swigging bottle after bottle of Mexican lager as we went through the motions squeezed onto the club's cosy stage.

"That ain't jazz!" said the belligerent veteran bebop drummer Tommy Chase who was going on next. It was obvious that only a handful of people had attempted the long trek to this far off corner of East Greenwich. Not even the girlfriend who had described our music as 'professional'. Indeed, the biggest applause of the night went to another support act, Frank Chickens, a pair of kooky Japanese performance artists who had a minor hit with a song called *We Are Ninja*.

Depressingly, our final gig would be the far from salubrious Lewisham Labour Club (my former Small Print band mates Mick and Alex would surely have approved), where a work colleague's 15-year-old brother turned up only to comment that we were "a pile of shit". To be fair to the lad, we all probably knew the game was up by then.

On stage that night I was wearing ripped vintage Levi's jeans with a hand-tailored fake leopard skin waistcoat, a 'soul brother' baker boy cap and a ridiculous polka-dot tie. I was turning a few heads but, deep down inside, I had had more than enough of chasing the vacuous trends of the day.

I myself had become that c**t in a clown suit.

Looking further beyond my immediate orbit, people were taking Ecstasy and dancing to Balearic beats and had got into the strange habit of hugging each other on the dance floor, as if they were long lost siblings. This was a far cry from posing at The Wag Club, as people were doing six months earlier. Peace and love were in the air.

The shifting social environment was certainly no place for a five-piece guitar pop outfit who wrote melodic three-and-a-half-minute songs about bad honeymoons and being left hanging on the end of telephone lines. Approaching the age of 24, I had a lot of growing up to do. I made my plans and told the guys to start looking around for other guitar players.

I enrolled on a teacher training course with the idea of working abroad to teach English as a Foreign Language. With English increasingly the world's *lingua franca*, there seemed to be opportunities galore for young native speakers like me to go out there and forge exciting new lives. Would I be heading for the dusty plains of Castille, in Spain, or a languid French university town? Or would I consider one of those Italian industrial powerhouses in Piedmont or Lombardy? As the Italian girl I had met on the induction course suggested, there would be both beaches and skiing in between the none too taxing bouts of teaching, not to mention legions of doe eyed, olive-skinned girls like her. Where exactly do I sign? I wondered.

Wherever my eventual destination, going abroad would spell the end of my endless ducking and diving and the start of something new. Soho, Covent Garden, Camden and all those other London hotspots would just have to get by without me for now.

After many false starts and several blind alleys things finally seemed to be on the turn. I would, in all seriousness, be embarking on a professional and grown-up career that, hopefully, would sustain me beyond my twenties. The kind of career mum and dad could confidently drop into conversations with their friends or neighbours.

One day I would make them proud.

16.

LET'S GET LOST

The summer of 1988 is remembered by some as the dawn of a new cultural and social phenomenon that was sweeping the nation: Acid House. Almost overnight the elitist clubs with their strict door policies and smart dress codes had become old hat.

Instead, clubbers got a brand-new beat from Chicago, Detroit, New York and Ibiza. Worshippers gathered *en masse* in disused warehouses and other off the grid spaces – car parks, motorway service stations, even fields – sweating it out all night in their uniform of baggy tie-dyed t-shirts, high top trainers and bucket hats.

Out on the dancefloor, bottled Czech lager gave way to water and Lucozade. The drug Ecstasy was all the ravers needed to get the party started. And in this dayglo coloured smiley-faced age of 'Aceeeed!', posing self-consciously in the shadows was no longer an option. All you had to do was *Jak Your Body, Break 4 Love* and head to the *Promised Land*.

I was blissfully unaware of such goings on and, having left my various cash-in-hand jobs and relieved myself from duties with 'The Paradise', I was now pretty much off the grid myself. Having journeyed the entire length of France in my ancient Peugeot hatchback, Petra and I had reached the northern Spanish port of Barcelona, installing our few worldly belongings into a tiny sixth storey attic flat at the very edge of the old city.

The flat was reached by climbing over 150 stairs which had us and our visitors – including the *butanero* (gas man) and his clunky orange cylinders – gasping for breath at the top.

Inside were plain whitewashed walls, a wonky brown tiled floor and one low ceilinged bedroom whose French windows led to a tight and vertiginous balcony. The view from here was an urban panorama of faded brown and green window blinds overshadowed by an army of spindly aerial masts. We didn't need a television. Instead, we could clearly observe our new neighbours as if they were characters in a minor soap opera trapped in similarly cramped living quarters.

The dissonant noises rising up from the street below – the constant rolling and unrolling of shop shutters, the clunking of gas cylinders, the jackpot machine from the bar that played *The Birdie Song* on repeat – were at first annoying yet quickly became part of the everyday soundscape. One morning we were awoken by the piercing sound of a bugle. Stepping out onto the balcony to see what was behind this commotion, we watched open mouthed as a ragged band of Roma gypsies ran the length of our street pushing a cart which housed a huge speaker and a cheap electronic keyboard which had been pre-programmed to belt out the popular melody *Cuando Cuando Cuando*. One of the gypsies was ahead of the cart holding what looked like an enormous scaffolding pole, and at the very top of the pole's shaft stood was balanced a petrified looking billy goat. Now that, I thought to myself, is how you make an entrance!

Other than a raised double bed made from chipped and crumbling MDF, our flat contained no furniture. At least not until some London friends arrived for a holiday. A lot of our friends appeared over the course of that summer, crashing willingly on a mattress on the sloping floor in the back. Our resourceful pair of holidaymakers helped furnish it with some prize skip finds they had found on their urban travels including a circular *fin de siècle* marble topped bar table and an elegant faux snakeskin sofa which we re-painted in pure white emulsion.

Me and Petra, a girlfriend I had met after she donated some old clothes and furniture to my regular Sunday market stall in Greenwich, were taking an optimistic leap into the future. Not only with our newfound relationship but also with this most dramatic change of lifestyle.

Neither of us had jobs lined up but we were hungry enough to exploit whatever contacts we had already made and were prepared to knock on doors and show our worth.

As someone with no previous teaching experience I had made the mistake of arriving towards the very end of the academic year. This is a time when the Spanish summer really begins to hot up and the students disappear for the long holiday that comes to an end only in late September. Most language school directors would not be looking to employ any new academic staff until the autumn.

My funds, which amounted to some cash plus a few traveller's cheques, were limited. So having paid our landlady a deposit, I had just enough to pay the monthly rent and feed myself on a diet of tuna and fried tomato pasta or the occasional *menu del dia* in the restaurant down in the square.

After a few frustrating weeks of phoning around in my non-existent Spanish using a local call box, I managed to secure a few teaching hours here and there, notably at a paper factory in the Zona Franca and then with an intense one-to-one class off the elegant Paseo de Gracia. My student had the noble face of a Conquistador but spoke so slowly and with such solemnity, I had to fill myself with cup after cup of *café cortado* just to stay awake.

The car broke down on the way back from the Costa Brava one weekend and was impounded by the police for a parking violation. I had to pay a 50,000 peseta fine just to release it which blew another hole into our already shaky finances. Our very first visitor, an eccentric Englishman called Barney who, among other things, taught me the brilliant swimming pool game Underwater Name That Tune, helped to push the stricken vehicle home. In the searing midday heat we somehow got all it the way from the car pound to the end of our street.

Our Ciutat Vella neighbourhood, which was slowly being transformed into the internationally renowned tourist centre it is today,* certainly had its rough and ready side. The dueño of a neighbourhood café, presumably a lifelong smoker, spoke through a gadget which he pressed against his

*As host city to the 1992 Olympic Games, Barcelona had a $9 billion makeover of its landmarks and infrastructure. As a result of the games, levels of tourism rose from £1.7m a year in 1990, peaking at £12m in 2019.

larynx which made him sound like a Dalek.

Meanwhile, a thick set brute with a pronounced limp would leer suggestively at Petra every time she exited the building's flimsy front door. Another local ne'er-do-well was seen disappearing into the labyrinth of dark medieval alleyways behind our building carrying two sizeable suitcases belonging to Petra's friends who had also come to visit. The two girls had been waiting in the street for us when the man had offered to help them.

"Si, si, si, tengo las maletas," admitted the tall Moroccan man, known in the noisy, hash-scented bar opposite as Ali, once I eventually tracked him down at his flat.

"Muchas gracias," I said, hoping the encounter wouldn't end badly.

"Aqui tienes, los estaba cuidando para tus amigas," he added with a winning smile, before calmly handing me the two hard suitcases over the doorway. Our friends, meanwhile, were somewhat relieved to discover that only a few items of underwear and some toiletries were missing. I had to admire the audacity of this operator.

As temperatures soared throughout June and July (our low-slung roof was pretty good at absorbing the sun's unceasing rays), we immersed ourselves further into the cultural life of the Catalan capital with its proud flags and strange language which, on the page, looked like French but spoken out loud sounded almost Germanic.

I took some free Spanish classes at a school, where I was briefly employed, at the top of the famous Ramblas. I learnt the differences between the two verbs 'to be' *soy* and *estar* and could identify different members of the family (*padre, madre, hijo…cuñado!*) while identifying both regular and irregular verbs.

In the break, I would sit at a table outside the Café Zurich in the Placa de Catalunya. This place seemed to be the very epicentre with its terrace bar tables occupied by local artists, flaneurs and itinerant EFL teachers like me, waited on by white tunicked waiters under its distinctive candy-striped sun canopy.

Our arrival in Barcelona via the border that cuts through the French Pyrenees Orientales and the long straight road that crosses the hinterland of the Costa Brava, coincided with a frenzied revival of Catalan culture following the death of Generalissimo Franco just a decade earlier. In the interests of nationalism following the brutal Civil War (1936-39), the long serving dictator had suppressed local cultures and languages throughout the regions of Spain, but these were now back in full bloom.

You could get by on the streets with a smattering of *castellano* Spanish – which I was struggling to master by day – but the most respected newspapers, magazines, television programmes, plays and movies were increasingly in the Catalan language.

Far from taking all their musical cues from English speaking America or Britain, the Catalans seemed to have their own musical heroes such as the folk singers Lluis Lllach and Joan Manuel Serrat, both of whom had been around since the 1960s. And with the regional government, the Generalitat de Catalunya, offering financial incentives for musicians to write, perform and record in the Catalan language, a new Rock Català scene was flourishing. The Catalans even had their own brand of flamenco music, Rumba Catalana, which was introduced to the city by poor migrants from the south who lived largely in the Raval neighbourhood.

Practically every week there seemed to be a new cultural spectacle laid on right in front of us: *sardanas,* the traditional Catalan dance accompanied by a woodwind band, in front of the old cathedral; young men forming impossibly high human towers (*castells*) outside City Hall and *gegants*, the alarmingly tall processional giants which depicted religious, historical and political personalities.

That the locals fiercely championed their folkloric customs and proudly retained their long-held traditions became abundantly clear to us when we began to hear the sound of firecrackers echoing in the street below. Every day the bangs became increasingly louder and more alarming, until I began to wonder if – as in George Orwell's document of Spain's Civil War, *Homage To Catalonia* – there was another outbreak of street violence between the Nationalists and their Republican enemies.

Fortunately, the cacophony turned out to be nothing more than a signal for the start of the Sant Joan festival, celebrated every June to mark the summer solstice.

The build-up seemed to last forever but, when Sant Joan eventually came, the night itself was a riot of pounding drums and handheld fireworks. Groups of playful youths dressed in colourful horned smocks held what looked like super-sized Catherine Wheels on tall sticks. It made our own Bonfire Night celebrations back home look like a pub bore doing a match trick.

The festival ended with a spectacular free outdoor concert in front of the mighty domes of Montjuic Castle. People were drinking sparkling *cava* from plastic glasses or, like us, sharing the wine from a bottle. We danced and sang along as best we could to the corny Latino pop played by a slick and highly entertaining live band.

I had been lucky enough to be present at some seminal live shows including The Smiths at the 'Jobs for a Change' festival and I witnessed The Beastie Boys rockin' da house at The Astoria. I had surged to the front for Trouble Funk's muscular, sweat-soaked performance at the Town and Country Club and had lost my voice joining in on the band's 'Ho-o's!', 'Say what's!' and 'Hell yeah's!'. As a student DJ, I had even persuaded the strictly non-dancing goths (unless it was for The Cure) to abandon their sticky floor for yet another joyous spin of *Free Nelson Mandela*. But, on this majestic hill rising to the east of the old city centre, I had never felt part of such a passionate, united and spirited display in my life.

And as that unforgettable summer rolled on, I found more teaching hours in a smart air-conditioned language school opposite Gaudi's *Casa Mila* on the Paseo de Gracia. I bought some swimming trunks in the Corte Inglés sale and at weekends we took the coastal train out to the beaches at Sitges or Sant Pol de Mar where we worked on our tans and slowly got through the pile of paperback books we had brought with us: *Nights At The Circus*, *The Bonfire of the Vanities*, *The New York Trilogy* and *The Unbearable Lightness of Being*.

Closer to the flat was La Barceloneta, which was a mere 10-minute walk away via the faded grandeur of the El Born neighbourhood and the ghostly abandoned Estacion de Francia. Here we encountered a scruffy urban beach which our neighbour upstairs had warned us was littered with the discarded needles of street whores and heroin addicts. We trod carefully over the hot sand then, managing to avoid being impaled by the drug paraphernalia, I launched myself into the Med only to come face to face with an enormous, bloated rat which bobbed lifelessly up and down on the murky brown water.

Still inhabited by loud gypsies and a few gnarly old fishermen, La Barceloneta's saving grace was a strip of long established *chiringuitos*. Each offered fresh seafood, enormous dishes of paella and delicious ice cream served up inside real frozen lemons. We became good pals with some Glaswegian architects who lived in the more respectable barrio of Gracia and I dusted down my oversized pinstriped Commes des Garcons jacket to join them at a chic bar where we drank impossibly tall glasses of vodka and tonic. We befriended Francisco, the bar's debonair owner, who greeted us both with an obsequious bow. We were true outsiders now and loving every minute of it. I sent a postcard to Gavin depicting a colourful montage of Gaudi's famous Sagrada Familia church. I felt I just had to update him with my news.

Hola Gavin!
We have been here a few weeks now, and I have had two job
interviews. One is for a summer school in the mountains staying in a
4-star hotel – no expenses!
We also found a flat!!
Let me know if anything comes of the video we did back in April.
I don't suppose it's been edited yet? Remember, I can dust down the
old guitar and be there like a shot if anything happens.
Love and best wishes, Dan x

High summer gave way to September and a slight dimming of the ever-present sun. It wouldn't be long now until I would be knocking on the doors of the city's language schools with my increasingly impressive CV. But my escape was interrupted one morning by the discovery of a note from Teléfonica. A telegram had arrived with my name on it and was awaiting collection at the central telephone exchange.

Sensing that this may be something quite important, I took the note and then walked quickly out of the main door and up through the twisting back streets of our humble *barrio*.

I passed the palm trees and the elegant cinema in the Placa

d'Urquinaona then arrived at the impressive modernist edifice that housed Teléfonica's headquarters just off the Placa de Catalunya.

Inside, long queues had formed at the various desks positioned all over the echoey marble hall. Whether buying some tomatoes at the local *mercado* or making a simple cash deposit in the bank, there were always queues to contend with in Spain. It must have been something to do with the strictly observed *siesta* whereby everything closed at lunchtime and then reopened slowly again in the late afternoon.

Eventually I reached the front of the queue marked 'Telegramas' and I was handed a small piece of paper which read simply:

DAN
GRANNIE DIED YESTERDAY. PLEASE PHONE HOME.
MUM AND DAD
[TELEGRAM END]

It was Grannie Squirrel. From a reverse charged call at a public phone box outside, dad's calm and friendly voice told me she had been briefly unwell and then was found unresponsive by a neighbour. It had been quick and painless he had reassured me. I was to attend the funeral the following week.

Grannie Squirrel had, I suppose, led a pretty good life. Unlike so many others of her generation she had got through a large part of the tumultuous twentieth century unscathed. In her time, there had been two world wars, the rise of fascism and communism in Europe followed by the Cold War, the Space Race, jet travel, the decline of the British Empire, the sexual revolution, the counterculture and, no doubt to her utter delight, the end of the Soviet Union.

As I gazed out of the aeroplane window as it circled over the browning fields around Gatwick Airport, I reflected on my own achievements, or lack of them, during this near quarter of a century spent on this planet. And if there was a tangible inventory for such a milestone, what could I possibly produce as evidence?

A litany of mostly dead-end jobs and a handful of relationships that, in the end, came to nothing would be the first that sprung to mind. But seeing things in a 'glass half full' kind of way, I had at least navigated the choppy waters of adolescence and was beginning to say *adios* to my somewhat shallow and often self-destructive lifestyle.

And, more importantly, I had survived.

Others hadn't been quite so lucky. When you are in your late teens and early twenties you feel invincible and yet there are dangers lurking around every corner. No-one should ever take their friends for granted.

Alex had of course departed this life, as had another good friend Tom. Tom studied Photography at my polytechnic and had taken some brilliant early promotional photos for the band. His tragically short life ended after he was run down by a motorcycle courier on Oxford Street. It was broad daylight.

And while I myself had seen off several sticky moments on the roads and survived pre and post-AIDS promiscuity, the misuse of amphetamines and other daft recreational drugs, the very worst that had happened to me was my meeting with the devil in the back streets of Amsterdam.

Weeks and even months after witnessing those demons I was noticeably withdrawn and distant. Friends noticed that I wasn't quite myself. I continued to suffer recurring panic attacks, with each one reminding me only too well of the full-blown horror of this episode.

Even the most innocuous situations would trigger these off; a crowded, noisy pub or a packed Underground platform would set me on some unstoppably grim train of thought. To the alarm of my companions, I would simply rush for the exit and then hide somewhere until my agitated state of mind and frantic breathing patterns returned to normal.

I never once told my family about them.

So, paranoid delusions aside, whatever *did* happen to the teenage dream? That dream I had harboured since being dazzled by the glare of Björn's star guitar as a ten-year-old. The very same dream that made me take a wrong turn down Devil Gate Drive only to end up in the nihilistic clutches of punk and new wave. As both a fan and a musical artist, I had gone on to witness the very best and the very worst that the 1980s could throw at me, yet had still refused to pack it all in.

Had I waved a white flag on pop stardom prematurely? Would Gavin and his Stranger Than Paradise pop-tastic splinter group

Don't Tell Dan! prove that I had walked out at the very moment of payback? I doubt it.

But being part of a band, this gang of creative souls and misfits who initially joined me in some innocent and joyful music making, and then on a doomed mission to storm the pop charts, certainly helped me to get back on track. Okay, so our three-and-a-half-minute songs didn't exactly light up the world but, for everyone involved, our shared venture provided thrills, spills and plenty of laughs along the way. We had thought big and had aimed for the stars. We could hold our heads up high.

However, committing to one all-encompassing creative project with all the sacrifices and sheer hard graft involved in making it work proved to be a trap. I would never get those 10,000 hours back and still wonder how I could have better spent this prime time of my youth.

Oh, hang the blessed DJ! Or, in my case, the blessed guitar pop band. Because the music that they constantly played said nothing to me about my life. And while hoping the success of Stranger Than Paradise would provide an antidote to my unconvincing start in life, I found that as we got nearer to our goal, I wanted it less.

As our lofty ambitions edged closer to grim reality, I tried too hard to fall in with other people's expectations and, in the process, completely lost sight of myself.

Now, in this lively and unpretentious *barrio* under the revealing Spanish sun, I was beginning to see myself a lot more clearly. For once in my life there would be no band mates, no photo shoots, no mindless ligging, no 'toilet circuit', no dodgy DJ's, no 'Next Big Thing' and *definitely* no fake leopard skin print waistcoat.

17.

DON'T YOU FORGET
ABOUT ME

I'm standing on a stage squeezed between a drum kit and a sharp-edged electric piano. I clutch my electric guitar and squint into the fluorescent glare as a sea of smiling faces gazes back. Over to the right I spy a young man pointing a professional film camera at us. A tall, middle-aged guy in what looks like a flak jacket is crouching down at the singer's feet taking photos of us.

Only a few minutes earlier I was backstage signing copies of our new LP and shaking hands with someone from Heart FM. A gang of very tipsy secretaries to my left are swaying merrily along to our walk-on theme *Mission Impossible*. This makes a change from my typical Friday night at home with a chilled glass of Viognier and a rock doc on BBC4.

"Good evening, we are Daniel Takes A Train!" announces our singer, Paul, who, because of the harsh stage lighting, already has beads of sweat running down his neck.

"Woo-hooo!" roars the crowd appreciably. Two dads from my son's school are wearing identical Daniel Takes A Train t-shirts. One of them is holding up the album and giving me a thumbs up sign.

James plays a lightning drum roll on his kit and then we're all in. I'm now strumming the chords to a song I wrote when I was 19 years old called *Will You Remember?*

When all is said and done
In future years to come
Will you remember?

I'm 55 years old now and am married with two children but, fortunately, I can still recall these simple chord progressions on the guitar fretboard. My simple D shape then moves to Em and back again. The girls packed in tightly at the front are swaying in time to the music as the breezy sax playing joins in. You know what, this rock and roll lark is a cinch. I never thought I'd be able to pick this up again. Yep, I've really missed being in the band.

So how did this most unlikely of musical renaissances happen?

Well, it all began in 2018 when our drummer, James, received a message via his personal YouTube channel. Would the band like to submit a track for a forthcoming compilation album to be released by the boutique label Firestation Records in Berlin, Germany?

The label's boss and huge indie pop devotee Uwe Weigmann had just seen the video for our song *I Don't Want This Love To Last Forever,* which James had uploaded on the content sharing platform, and he liked it. Up until then, the original VHS copy of the track had only been seen by only a handful of people connected with the band. Despite the fact I had both written, arranged and performed the song, I had never once possessed a version of my own.

Anyway, Daniel Takes A Train's music was perfect for Firestation, explained Weigmann, who championed mostly British guitar pop bands from the 1980s and early 1990s – the ones that sounded as if they might have made it back in the day, but for one reason or another didn't.

Amazing news, we agreed unanimously, once James had managed to track us all down. Speaking for myself, I had long since put to bed any dreams of indie credibility and didn't even play the guitar much. Work and family with the responsibility of having young children accounted for most of my time and energy. Still, I was up for a bit of an adventure and would be able to put my newly acquired skills as a film music composer to the test.

During our three-decade-long hiatus, singer Paul had written Eurovision song entries for Slovenia as well as *Sing For England*, an official 2012 World Cup song. Less successfully he had been rejected at the audition stage for *Britain's Got Talent* with a rendition of *Beyond The Sea* dressed as a naval officer. Meanwhile, original bassist Rupert had been both managing and playing bass guitar with a disco party outfit in the Nottingham area. Drummer James hadn't exactly given up either. He was in a weekend weddings band which specialised in renditions of Baby Boomer classics such as *Sweet Caroline* and *Hi Ho Silver Lining*.

Of course, we were only too delighted for our track to be listed on the new CD alongside other mid-1980s nearly-rans; Chinese Gangster Element, The Dancing Bears and Ten Million Quentins.

But wait a minute, suggested Paul, who since the band had split up had never quite accepted that the pop game was up. What if we were to send the Berlin indie label some of the other tracks we had recorded during the period we were active? After all, Daniel Takes A Train and their precursors Illicit Kiss had recorded several studio demos between the years 1984 and 1988. These were roundly rejected by record industry insiders at the time but surely these had some artistic and commercial merit, he argued.

We scratched our heads. Did any of these recordings still exist? And, if so, how many of them were there? And, more importantly, were these recordings of a reasonable enough quality to be committed to CD or even vinyl?

We searched our lofts and raided moth-infested trunks and dusty drawers in an effort to find the original masters, which had been recorded on 16 and 24 track reel-to-reel tape.

Incredibly, these analogue artefacts representing four or five separate recording sessions in the 1980s were still intact. Subsequently, the band had a meeting over Skype then reached the conclusion that we had at least 16 listenable tracks in total – enough to release a complete album under our own name.

When Paul relayed the news back to Berlin, the people at Firestation were delighted and immediately set about putting together our debut album *Style, Charm and Commotion*. Most copies of this limited-edition vinyl LP would be sold to fans in Japan where, even today, there remains an enormous interest in jangle and indie pop re-releases.

So Daniel Takes A Train's one and only vinyl album was released in August 2018 – almost exactly 30 years after the band had split up.

Picking up on this unusual story with its underlying themes of friendship, failure, resilience and eventual redemption, the media had their brief feeding frenzy.

Halfway through one of my Media Studies classes, I was interrupted by a reporter from *The Times*. I sneaked out into the hallway so I could take the call. "So, Dan," she asked. "How *did* the band start?" '80s Band Pop Back for a Shot at Stardom,' ran their headline the very next day.

In one crazy week the band appeared on both national and local television channels as well as dozens of radio stations. Paul even persuaded a film crew to visit his house in Blackheath where Channel 5 News put together a feature on us.

"If we were nineteen again, I'm sure we would go absolutely mad," I remarked to the interviewer on camera. "It really would be sex, drugs and rock and roll. The trouble is, I've got to disappear now in order to pick up my daughter from a sleepover!"

Such was the genuine and heartfelt interest in our story that we had little option but to reform. But some things are easier said than done.

During a disastrous first rehearsal, cues were missed, lyric lines forgotten and any basic stage craft we might have once had went completely AWOL. For us ageing part-timers it was a cruel reminder there was work to do. With our comeback gig in central London just a matter of weeks away, we were beginning to feel the heat.

Enter manager, Jon Mellor, an old business acquaintance of Paul who, meeting us for the first time in the Blackheath branch of Café Rouge, immediately suggested the band enlist the services of Andy Rourke formerly of The Smiths.

"That would be awesome," I said, "but we already have the services of two bass players. Anyway, do you really think he'd want to rehearse in New Cross with us?"

"I'll run it by him," said Jon, "Andy's living in New York these days but I'm sure he could be persuaded to fly over."

"Oh, okay, well let me know how it goes."

"I could also get you Peter Hook," he then suggested nonchalantly, chewing on some recently arrived garlic flatbread. "Have a think."

A lot of what Jon said made very little sense indeed, in particular his proposed trip to Oslo to appear live on a popular breakfast television show.

"All bands should do Norwegian breakfast telly," he said, tucking into his Demi Poulet. "The Norwegians are very appreciative people. They'll treat you like kings."

But whatever my reservations about his character, here was someone who seemed to be genuinely excited by our little band. If only we'd had someone like him around back in the day, we all thought. The music business is a fickle one at best and to get anywhere you need front, which is pretty much the same as telling lies or half-truths. Jon and his curious brand of blue-sky thinking could do our bidding for us this time. We would just get on with the music.

He hired a film crew to make a rockumentary about us and he dropped some impressive industry names, giving us the idea that these individuals would be in the audience at our shows. One of these contacts, he maintained, was interested in using our song *I Don't Want This Love To Last Forever* for a major television and radio ad campaign. As co-writer of the song, I was set to make a small fortune. It was certainly a distraction being a university lecturer and freelance journo one minute and the next a rich and successful pop composer.

Jon even called me personally to advise me on the direction of my solo career, (a solo career, of course! why didn't I think of that before?), setting me up with a couple of singers who were last seen inhabiting the lower regions of indie charts, circa 2006. "You're the chief songwriter, Dan, so don't worry about the others. Think about yourself."

Of course, our manager's many deceptions soon unravelled, especially after the proposed tour with Squeeze and the week-long recording session at Abbey Road failed to materialise.

The man needed a team of qualified mental health care professionals, not a group of over-excited men in their fifties who could only see one last shot at fame.

At one point there was even a bizarre plan to have Paul singing a duet with Marc Almond, who was going to hot foot it over from the O2 to our intimate cellar gig in West London. Then there was the proposed 1980s sophisti-pop supergroup featuring members of Halo James, Blue Mercedes and The Lotus Eaters to be produced by someone who was in The Associates. What? I began to wonder where I fitted into to all of this.

Thankfully we rose above this madness and held things together for long enough to perform in front of a sell-out crowd one hot September evening at The Troubadour, the legendary west London venue where Dylan, Hendrix and members of Led Zeppelin once played.

As Adam Ant so eloquently sung on his hit *Prince Charming*, 'ridicule is nothing to be scared of.' Indeed, the night proved to be such a rip-roaring success that we decided to extend our musical journey further, going on to play some more club gigs and then write some brand-new songs, which ended up on our self-released album *Last Ticket To Tango* in 2021. Coincidentally, the album's producer was the late Pat Collier who once played bass in The Vibrators, the punk band responsible for *Baby Baby*, the single I reluctantly bought from a friend way back in 1977.

But these days, mainstream success is even harder to come by than it was in the 1980s and, like many under-the-radar artists, we must play the long game of pop. 'Content is king', I am repeatedly told. And so, in the spirit of Bill Gates's mantra, we continue to release our tunes on Spotify and other digital platforms in the hope that we get picked up by DJ's, influencers and, with luck, the biggest-hitting play listers.

Admittedly, the financial rewards are nothing to get excited about. Coldplay and Adele certainly won't be losing sleep over our sales figures, yet the band has built a sizeable online following since getting back together. Our ska-tinged pop single *Sleeping With The Enemy*, about a KGB agent who defects to the West, has been streamed over

150,000 times, and we even managed a Top 3 hit in Mike Read's Heritage Chart with our single *Be Happy* in January 2024. Not bad, considering the single was competing alongside seasoned chart veterans such as Cher, Take That and The Pogues. It's rewarding to think that, right now, there are thousands of new listeners out there still waiting to discover Daniel Takes A Train. Music, it would seem, has still got a hold on us.

And despite all that we've been through, we're still friends. We don't always share the same taste in bands, clothes, films or politics, but we still pop over to each other's houses to jam. We're still recording and releasing new material.

All these decades later, we truly believe we can write the perfect pop song.

ACKNOWLEDGEMENTS

I would like to thank the following people for helping this book come to fruition.

Elizabeth Macdonald, Guy Gausden, Sheena Macdonald and Dr Thembi Mutch offered helpful and highly insightful critiques of my earliest drafts. Genevieve Fox gave my rough manuscript the equivalent of a 2024 digital remaster, helping me to turn what was a collection of writings on life and music into a more coherent and focused memoir. Thanks also to Ray Connolly, author of *That'll Be The Day*, whose kind words persuaded me to write something about my own teenage years.

And, as I spent large amounts of time inhabiting my own distant past, I was encouraged and supported all the while by my amazing and understanding wife, Miranda.

Finally, I'd like to dedicate this book to my fellow band members and musical collaborators, past and present. It's been a long old road from the school triangle orchestras and brass bands to Daniel Takes A Train, and all those other promising yet short lived outfits I have so far been involved in: BBC5, Small Print, Zero Beat, Illicit Kiss, El Mundo de Pino, Fever and Who Shot Liberty? to name just a few. I sincerely hope everyone involved in these projects has fond memories of our time together. Music is fundamental to our lives and, whatever our ambitions or skills level, the process of making it remains a powerful and meaningful way of connecting with other human beings.

ABOUT THE AUTHOR

After a four-year stint as lead guitarist with pop wannabes Daniel Takes A Train, Dan Synge taught English in Barcelona and London before becoming a journalist, going on to freelance for *The Guardian*, the *Financial Times*, the *Independent* and *Time Out*.

He has worked for a number of consumer magazines and websites including *Esquire*, where he wrote about discovering the 'West Pole' in a remote part of the Galapagos Islands. As an independent publisher and editor, he has launched both local luxury lifestyle magazines and illustrated travel guides.

Dan has combined a career in journalism and publishing with being a senior university lecturer teaching Journalism and Media Studies. He returned to music making following his band's surprise rediscovery by a German record label in 2018.

His other books include *Cool Collectables* (Mitchell Beazley) and *The Survival Guide to Journalism* (McGraw Hill).

He lives in London and is married with two children.

If you enjoyed the time and the place of this story, why not listen to this author curated playlist featuring some of the songs mentioned in the book.

The Playlist **Whatever Happened to the Teenage Dream?**
includes tracks by T Rex, ABBA, Cat Stevens, Penetration, Prefab Sprout, Scritti Politti and many more

https://open.spotify.com/playlist/7kOuJP3mPOeHBLlpgSQV99?si=598fd64f30e94860

Printed in Great Britain
by Amazon

50979215R00118